———INVITATI
God's Calling for

Other books by Francis Dewar:

Live for a Change: Discovering and Using Your Gifts
(DLT 1988)

Called or Collared? An Alternative Approach to Vocation
(SPCK 1991)

Give Yourself a Break
(Hunt & Thorpe 1992)

—INVITATIONS—
God's Calling for Everyone

Stories and quotations
to illuminate a journey

Francis Dewar

First published in Great Britain 1996

Society for Promoting Christian Knowledge
36 Causton Street
London SW1P 4ST

AUTHOR'S NOTE
It has been decided to retain the American spelling
where quotations are by American authors.
In many cases, also, exclusive language remains unchanged,
to avoid too much alteration of authors' original words.

British Library Cataloguing-in-Publication Data
A catalogue record of this book is available from
the British Library

ISBN 978–0–281–04948–6

10

Typeset by Pioneer Associates, Perthshire
Printed in Great Britain by
The Cromwell Press, Melksham, Wiltshire
Subsequent digital printing in Great Britain by
Ashford Colour Press Ltd, Gosport, Hampshire

Produced on paper from sustainable forests

Contents

*In gratitude for Elizabeth O'Connor
and for her writings*

This book will make a traveller of thee,
If by its counsel thou wilt rulèd be,
It will direct thee to the Holy Land,
If thou wilt its directions understand:
Yea, it will make the slothful active be;
The blind also delightful things to see.

John Bunyan, The Pilgrim's Progress

Introduction

The mud-spattered mail-coach was labouring slowly up Shooter's Hill in the darkness on its way to Dover one Friday night in November 1775 when a lone horseman from London galloped up with an urgent message for a Mr Lorry. The recipient read it, and the reply he gave to the messenger to take back was just three words, 'Recalled to life'.

The coach lumbered on again . . .

> 'Tom!' softly over the coach roof.
> 'Hallo, Joe.'
> 'Did you hear the message?'
> 'I did, Joe.'
> 'What did you make of it, Tom?'
> 'Nothing at all, Joe.'
> 'That's a coincidence, too,' the guard mused, 'for I
>   made the same of it myself.'

As Charles Dickens's story (*A Tale of Two Cities*) unfolds, we discover the message refers to one Dr Manette who has been in prison in France for many years without trial. Mr Lorry's mission is to bring him over to England and to freedom.

There are many ways of being imprisoned: by a job which you find irksome and in which you feel trapped; by society's expectations which require you to spend your time and your energy in ways that feel foreign to your true nature; by your nearest and dearest who expect you to conform to their notion of what you should do and the kind of person you should be; by what you feel to be flaws or handicaps in your own character and temperament; by your upbringing and the kind of background in which you were raised; by things that happen to you which restrict your freedom of movement, literally or metaphorically.

Almost any circumstances can *feel* like a prison. I personally felt that way at times about being an Anglican parish clergyman, which I was for more than twenty years. You might ask, 'Then why on earth did you stick it for so long?' Well, why *do* people stay in their prisons? It feels safer; opening a door and walking out of your prison can feel quite scary. Most people are frightened of real freedom. For myself, it took a long time even to face the fact that I felt in some ways imprisoned as a parish priest. I had gone into it very much from a sense of duty, impelled by the notion that being a Christian meant doing things you did not want to do: and that if you liked doing them they probably were not Christian!

So I have brought together this collection of stories and quotations in the hope that it will illuminate for you the adventure of being recalled (or called, as the case may be) to life. It is about calling or vocation in the sense of finding life, *joie de vivre*, and fruitfulness in some specific activity or piece of work which is yours to do in some unique way. Nowadays the word vocation is a currency so devalued as to be almost worthless. It trips off the tongues of politicians in phrases like vocational training or National Vocational Qualifications. By it they mean little more than a job, any job by which you can support yourself – one more cipher removed from the unemployment statistics. What a come-down for such a wonderful and ennobling notion, the idea that God values each individual so much that he has a personal invitation for each one of us: 'Come, I have a special task for you to do, something that you were born for, that will bring you untold fulfilment, through which others also may be freed or enriched or enlivened.'

I will say more about this personal dimension of vocation in a moment. First, I need to clear away some older misconceptions, in particular the restriction of the word vocation to certain professions, like clergy, doctors, nurses or teachers. That is a legitimate use of the word vocation but it is very narrow, and it carries with it various assumptions: that vocation means one of the professions; that it is lifelong; that it requires years of training; and that it is definitely not for ordinary folk. I believe the word vocation urgently needs rescuing from these connotations. Vocation, the calling of God, is, potentially, addressed to every human being. We all, whoever we are, however dull and unpromising we feel, have something of value to offer to life. We each have something special to do, just as each person's fingerprints are unique, and each human being's genetic code is different from everyone else's.

This is a difficult notion for some to grasp, because so much of our life is lived according to what is expected of us, and our idea of what vocation or calling means is very much coloured by this fact. Dennis Potter, the television playwright, reckoned we live in a karaoke culture where we are always singing someone else's song: 'Everything is written for you; and that is the way life appears to a lot of people.' If you live all of your life that way you are living in a kind of prison, even if you are not aware of it. It is a prison in the sense that it keeps your unique contribution, your own song as it were, under lock and key, well out of sight of both yourself and of other people. This may satisfy you for a time, but as you move through your thirties and forties, sooner or later there begin to be whispers from within that all is not well. All sorts of vague yearnings begin to be felt. If you listen long enough and carefully enough to these inner promptings they are often clues – admittedly sometimes no more than clues – to what your unique personal offering might be. Because, to continue Dennis Potter's metaphor, you have a song of your own to write and to sing, *your* words and *your* music.

We are talking here about what I would call your personal vocation, the unearthing of your hidden treasure which God invites you to mine from deep within yourself and to offer in some specific way. There is more to life than merely doing what is expected of you.

As you read this you may be thinking 'all this sounds fine, and I do sometimes wish that the things I have to do at work or at home engaged more of my genuine interest and enthusiasm. There ought somehow to be more to life. But what you are saying sounds altogether too adventurous for someone like me.' Most of us feel like that at times. Many factors conspire to convince us that we are not creative, that we are not special, that we have no particular ability, that life is risky enough without sticking our necks out unnecessarily. And yet, and yet . . . we cannot help admiring a courageous initiative taken by someone; or feeling encouraged by an uncalled-for act of kindness, or inspired by a friend's creativity. It seems that deep inside each of us is a longing for a better life, a better world. It may get focused on a new car, or the latest gadget, or next year's holiday. We may never get further than putting a weekly pound on the lottery. But however much we trivialize it or ignore it, there is this longing in us.

Once you have turned thirty, for both women and men, it can come to the surface in quite powerful ways. Usually these are oblique and camouflaged reminders from that longing centre deep within you, that you do in fact yourself have some contribution of your own to make to that better world. What you have to offer may not be spectacular; like the person in the office with a gift for listening who unobtrusively makes such a significant contribution to the feel of the place. It may not be noticed or even known about except by one or two others. If it is, it will not necessarily make you universally popular, like the member of a religious order who begins to discover what his or her personal calling is: people who live their personal calling are often disturbers of what passes for peace in this world, whatever the context. You will be fortunate if it is something you do as part of your paid work. It is more likely to be something you do in addition to earning your living, a sideline, an occasional activity, perhaps something that originally grew from a hobby. I think, for example, of one person whose lifelong interest in gardening led eventually to standing for the Green Party in a local election. Commonly it arises at the point of some trauma or problem or handicap which you have come to some sort of terms with, and which turns out, strangely, to be a profound gift. But whatever it is, it will be something you discover that you love to do, something that engages your energy and enthusiasm at a deep level.

Suggestions on how to use this book

This collection is designed to be a companion for you as you listen for what God may be inviting you to offer, that task, small or great, which is uniquely yours to do at this point in your life. I hope that as you reflect on the stories and quotations you will keep some kind of journal or jottings book in which you record your reactions; the feelings, hopes, dreams, longings, regrets, fears, anger, etc. that they evoke in you. Use them as a stimulus to become more aware of who you are; of your hopes for yourself and for the world; of where your real energies and enthusiasms draw you; of what you long for. This is not as easy as it sounds, 'I only wanted to live in accordance with the promptings which came from my true self. Why was that so difficult?' mused Emil, in Hermann Hesse's novel *Demian*. Most of us in our karaoke society are out of touch with our inner selves and our deeper possibilities. By the same token we are very deaf to what God wants us to do: many of us for all sorts of reasons have pretty distorted notions of who or what God is. So there are many factors involved. I have grouped the stories and quotations under seventeen headings. Each of the headings or themes has a place in the process of discerning your personal calling. Their order is not too important. You can start anywhere. It is best to start with what attracts or draws you most, though in the long run you will need to engage with each of these themes in one way or another. I see them all as separate threads being woven together to form a piece of cloth, the pattern of which only gradually becomes clear.

Accept your wounds and disabilities
Know yourself loved by God
Listen to your feelings
Be still and know
Count the cost
Seek wholeness
Know God

Hear a call
Dream dreams
Get into action
Face your fears
Know the world's needs
Get confirmation from others
Know your gifts and leanings

What God is inviting you to do does not usually become clear quickly, and it may well take months, or years, or even decades. Do not let that deter you. I remember one person who came on a course I ran who took another ten years to come to terms with the fact that she needed some counselling before she could be free enough even to begin to listen for God's beckoning. Nor does the need for you to work with each one of the threads ever completely cease. For example, who of us can say we truly know God? Who can claim to be fully conversant with the world's needs? How many of us are even fully aware of our own gifts? New ones are being offered to us day by day and year by year. To engage with each thread is itself to be involved in a journey; how much more is that true as you take time to let the threads be woven together, so that each is illuminated and clarified as it is related to the others. But only slowly does a pattern or picture begin to be discernible, the lineaments of what God is inviting you to do.

And, of course, the nature of your God-given task may itself change as the years pass. There is nothing fixed or final about God's personal invitation to you. It is not something settled once and for all. As you respond, God calls you on further. It is a continuous, lifelong process of growing in attentiveness and responsiveness. It is a giving of yourself in specific action in which you gradually grow in your willingness to move out, like Abraham in Genesis chapter 12, in response to God's calling, beyond the known ways and aside from the accepted methods.

One other preliminary point needs to be made. There are many levels, if that is the right word, of God's calling to us, addressing the many needs of our nature and the many stages in our lives. There are many needs that human beings have. The basic ones are for food, shelter, safety, love and esteem. But not all needs are for receiving. As our basic needs are met, we all need to be able to be generous, to give love, to be creative, and to have some opportunity to do what we are for. These 'higher' needs tend only to surface as more basic needs are met. If you ask typical school-leavers what they want – apart from winning the lottery! – it will be a job, a way of earning their living. Later it will be to settle down, to find a life partner, or a community to be part of. It is only when these needs and wants have to some extent been met that the deeper life questions which are the focus of this book tend to arise.

Etty Hillesum, the Dutch girl who died in Auschwitz in 1943, wrote in her diary:

> Looked at Japanese prints this afternoon . . . That's how I want to write. With that much space round a few words . . . If I should ever write – but what? – I would like to brush in a few words against a wordless background . . . What matters is the right relationship between words and wordlessness, the wordlessness in which much more happens than in all the words one can string together.

That is the spirit in which this collection is offered, pregnant stories and quotations which I hope will fructify the space in which they are suspended, like pictures on an empty wall. *Much more will happen in the space between them if you do not rush from one to the next, but take time to let each one take root within you.* This is not a book to read through at a sitting, but one to dip into; perhaps to go back again and again to quotations or stories that you find nourishing, and let them feed your spirit more deeply, until you begin to make them your own, as you experience what they speak of at first hand.

Francis Dewar
Kings Sutton

I

An invitation to live

I have come that you may have life, and have it to the full.

The Gospel of John

There is a board above the front door of an old house near where I live. On it is painted a sundial, with the Latin inscription *Dum vivimus vivamus*, which means 'While we live, let us *live*'. I like that. It might have been the title of this chapter. God's invitation to us is to live, a full-blooded generous living of our giftedness. That is what it is to sing your song, like the thrush that gives its all in the tree outside my window each day. We are to discover and to do what we most deeply love to do.

You may have very little idea of what that is. Many of us are out of touch with our inmost longings; we do not really know what we love to do except at a rather superficial level. In fact some of us have been taught from an early age that it is selfish to give any attention to our own wishes and desires. And so, as you thumb through this chapter, you may feel like Etty (p. 9), confused and directionless. I realize this is not a very comfortable position to be in. I should know: I have been in it many times myself. But potentially it is a very fruitful state to be in. The key is to be open, and not to allow yourself self-pity about your confusion. The great thing about being confused and not knowing where you are going is that it encourages you to be still, to listen and look, to open every pore expectantly, to play around with possibilities. People who know exactly where they are going and what they have to do *can* be a menace. Confidence that you are right is not a state of mind that makes for openness to God's leading. So take heart, and let Rilke's (p. 16) encouraging words about living the questions stay with you. Accept your confused state and be a bit more friendly to it. Listen for what your questions really are. What is it you want? What are

7

you looking for? Play with the images and metaphors of personal calling in this chapter:

> a song to be sung,
> a seed to germinate,
> an awakening from death to be experienced,
> a spark to be fanned into flame,
> a narrow road to be searched for.

Draw them; have conversations with them (put your questions and comments to them, and imagine what they reply); let them stimulate your own hopes and longings which may have been dormant for many years.

According to the legend, when Parsifal left home his mother told him not to ask any questions on his travels. Too many of us accept the way things are without question. We need to learn to ask questions. Jesus said that to enter the Kingdom of God we must become like little children. One of the most obvious characteristics of young children is that they ask questions, often the sort of penetrating and blunt questions we would rather they did not ask! For example, when you have a family and a large mortgage it is tempting to feel that certain questions are off limits. But there is no harm in asking them in the privacy of your own heart. And do not allow yourself to be seduced by the assumption that there is only one way to answer them. This is the spirit in which I have chosen the quotations in this section. One or two of them may be familiar, like, for example, the parable of the sower. Be open to the possibility that there may be more to it than meets the eye. As you read it you may dismiss it through overfamiliarity. But supposing the seed represents God's word to *you*, God's personal calling to *you* . . .?

Two questions to reflect on

- What brings you to life?
- What has a deadening effect on you?

Ask yourself these questions in all the circumstances of your daily life and work and leisure, in what you do, and in what you encounter, even in the smallest details of your existence. Begin to develop an awareness of what is life-giving for you, and what is deadening.

——— ✦ ———

There is an old Christian tradition
that God sends each person into this world
with a special message to deliver,
with a special song to sing for others,
with a special act of love to bestow.
No one else can speak my message,
or sing my song,
or offer my act of love.
These are entrusted only to me.

John Powell, *Through Seasons of the Heart* (Collins 1988)

It started last night; then the turbulence began to swirl up inside me, as vapour swirls up from a swamp . . . This morning everything seemed fine again. But when I began cycling down Apollolaan, there it was back, all the questioning, the discontent, the feeling that everything was empty of meaning, the sense that life was unfulfilled, all that pointless brooding. And right now I am sunk in the mire. And even the certain knowledge that this too will pass has brought me no peace this time . . . I still lack a basic tune; a steady undercurrent; the inner source that feeds me keeps drying up and, worse still, I think too much.

Etty Hillesum, *Etty: A Diary 1941–43* (Jonathan Cape 1983)

One of the challenges we all face is to be continually sensitive to the unfolding of God's plan in our lives: to give free and open assent to the destiny his love is shaping for us. It is so easy to lose that sensitivity. So much of our life is dominated by the mechanical, by the response that is expected or demanded of us, by attempts to predict or anticipate growth, that we are always in danger of losing contact with life as a mystery – and so with life itself. When we cease to respond to life with wonder we begin to understand it merely as a problem, a series of complicated interlocking processes. But our life is whole. And the wholeness is both its mystery and its simplicity.

John Main, *The Present Christ* (DLT 1985)

Though we may have only a tiny spark or smouldering wick within us, our task is to fan it into fire.

Elizabeth O'Connor, *Cry Pain, Cry Hope* (Word Inc. 1987)

Again [Jesus] began to teach by the lakeside, but such a huge crowd gathered round him that he got into a boat on the lake and sat there. The people were all along the shore, at the water's edge. He taught them many things in parables, and in the course of his teaching he said to them, 'Listen! Imagine a sower going out to sow. Now it happened that, as he sowed, some of the seed fell on the edge of the path, and the birds came and ate it up. Some seed fell on rocky ground where it found little soil and sprang up straightaway, because there was no depth of earth; and when the sun came up it was scorched and, not having any roots, it withered away. Some seed fell into thorns, and the thorns grew up and choked it, and it produced no crop. And some seeds fell into rich soil and, growing tall and strong, produced crop; and yielded thirty, sixty, even a hundredfold.' And he said, 'Listen, anyone who has ears to hear!' . . .

He said to them, 'Do you not understand this parable? Then how will you understand any of the parables? What the sower is sowing is the word. Those on the edge of the path where the word is sown are people who have no sooner heard it than Satan comes and carries away the word that was sown in them. Similarly, those who receive the seed on patches of rock are people who, when first they hear the word, welcome it at once with joy. But they have no root in them, they do not last; should some trial come, or some persecution on account of the word, they fall away at once. Then there are others who receive the seed in thorns. These have heard the word, but the worries of this world, the lure of riches and all the other passions come in to choke the word, and so it produces nothing. And there are those who have received the seed in rich soil: they hear the word and accept it and yield a harvest, thirty and sixty and a hundredfold.'

Mark 4.1–9; 13–20

Seed prematurely sown does not sprout.

Rainer Maria Rilke, *Letters to a Young Poet*
(W. W. Norton 1954)

Maybe sometimes you are aware of [the personal calling of God] in the brief twinkling it takes to decide whether to be honest or not at a particular moment in a conversation that seems to call for it or whether you take refuge in silence or in platitudes. Maybe sometimes you notice it in suddenly being aware, as you go about your daily activities, of a small kindness you could do or a contribution you could make: and you refrain, from the fear that you will make yourself vulnerable, 'I'll look foolish', or 'My offer may be rejected', or, 'So-and-so will undoubtedly misinterpret it'. Perhaps you have noticed it on a larger scale, in the beginnings of a desire to take some creative step, which you have acted on with a strong sense of inner rightness and peace: or which you have funked with the subsequent depressed feeling of having been basically untrue to yourself?

These are the kinds of ways you begin to be aware of God's personal calling; not usually in the grand gesture, but in these tiny daily opportunities to be truer to what you are and could be. As you begin to live a little more in this kind of way he will begin to call you to take more distinct and perhaps more noticeable initiatives, which then begin to be more identifiable to yourself and others as a calling from God. But writ large or writ small, the process is fundamentally the same. 'The longest journey starts with but a single step.' And however long the journey is, and however publicly visible it may be, subjectively it feels like just a step at a time . . .

This factor does make it quite difficult to speak about the personal calling of God. Our response to his personal calling is *always* in the moment, from moment to moment. The attempt to describe it is liable to falsify it by appearing to give it much too solid or permanent a quality; because when one describes it it is usually past. For example when you read what I am writing now it will be in black and white on a printed page. But as I write it, I do so haltingly, a phrase or sentence at a time on the trackless void of the paper in front of me. The feel of this to me is *totally* different from what it looks like to you. And so it is usually with responding to the personal calling of God.

Francis Dewar, *Called or Collared?* (SPCK 1991)

On the following day as John stood there again with two of his disciples, Jesus passed, and John stared hard at him and said, 'Look, there is the lamb of God'. Hearing this, the two disciples followed Jesus. Jesus turned round, saw them following and said, 'What do you want?'

John 1.35–8

When we succeed in ignoring our wants they either find expression in destructive ways or cause us all kinds of ills and problems that make us self-centered and self-serving – the very end we are so anxious to avoid. The outcome, however, is not usually this dramatic. Out of touch with the life-giving energy of our wants and desires, we are more apt to become flat and uninteresting people. Imperceptibly disintegration goes on at the very core of life. The calm and expressionless face reflects not peace at the center, but a dying going on within.

For these passionless selves the words were spoken, 'Awake, O sleeper, and arise from the dead, and Christ will give you light' (Eph. 5.14, RSV).

Elizabeth O'Connor, *Cry Pain, Cry Hope*

(As you read this quotation put yourself in the place of Lazarus. What kind of 'death' has you in its grip? Take a few minutes in silence to picture your tomb or prison, and yourself in it. Jesus comes and calls you to come out. What help do you need to do this? Ask him for it.)

There was a man named Lazarus who lived in the village of Bethany with the two sisters, Mary and Martha, and he was ill. It was the same Mary, the sister of the sick man Lazarus, who anointed the Lord with ointment and wiped his feet with her hair. The sisters sent this message to Jesus, 'Lord, the man you love is ill'.

On arriving, Jesus found that Lazarus had been in the tomb for four days already.

Mary went to Jesus, and as soon as she saw him she threw herself at his feet, saying, 'Lord, if you had been here, my brother would not have died'. At the sight of her tears, and those of the Jews who followed her, Jesus said in great distress, with a sigh that came straight from the heart, 'Where have you put him?' They said, 'Lord, come and see'. Jesus wept; and the Jews said, 'See how much he loved him!' But there were some who remarked, 'He opened the eyes of the blind man, could he not have prevented this man's death?' Still sighing, Jesus reached the tomb: it was a cave with a stone to close the opening. Jesus said, 'Take the stone away'. Martha said to him, 'Lord, by now he will smell; this is the fourth day'. Jesus replied, 'Have I not told you that if you believe you will see the glory of God?' So they took away the stone. Then Jesus lifted up his eyes and said:

'Father, I thank you for hearing my prayer.
I knew indeed that you always hear me,
but I speak
for the sake of all these who stand round me,
so that they may believe it was you who sent me.'

When he had said this, he cried in a loud voice, 'Lazarus, here! Come out!' The dead man came out, his feet and hands bound with bands of stuff and a cloth round his face. Jesus said to them, 'Unbind him, let him go free'.

John 11.1–3, 17, 32–44

To have life as vocation is to be aware that there are two ways to go – the wide road and the narrow road. The wide road might be called the way of unconsciousness and the narrow road the way of consciousness. The wide road is the road of the crowd. Jesus describes the people on it as not seeing and not hearing. They have an invitation to a banquet, but are too busy to attend. They always have something very important that needs to be done, and their reasons are always logical and convincing. They can explain well to others because they have explained well to themselves, silencing any murmurs of dissent that come from within. They have lost awareness that there are two ways. They respond to externals only, since their attention is outward. They have many answers. When they do ask questions they ask them of others but never themselves. There is a sameness about those in the crowd. By contrast with 'round characters' that develop and change, they are what in fiction writing is known as 'flat characters', which means that they do not change. They are the same at the end of the story as at the beginning. They do not receive anything into themselves; things happen to them, but never in them. Their lives are rich in outer events, and poor in inner ones. They are the impoverished who are not included in any poverty program. They are the dead who do not know they sleep.

Elizabeth O'Connor, *Journey Inward, Journey Outward*
(Harper & Row 1968)

On his death bed Rabbi Zuscha was asked what he thought life beyond the grave would be like. The old man thought for a long time: then he replied: 'I don't really know. But one thing I do know: when I get there I am not going to be asked "Why weren't you Moses?" or "Why weren't you David?" I am going to be asked "Why weren't you Zuscha?"'

Nasrudin was at the teahouse with some of his cronies. There was some discussion about life after death. Nasrudin seemed unusually silent. After a while one of them turned to him, 'Come on! You're supposed to be some kind of wiseacre: tell us: is there life after death?' 'It's people who don't know what to do with this life who want another that will last for ever,' said Nasrudin. 'Yes, but is there life after death or isn't there?' 'Is there life before death?' replied Nasrudin: 'that is the question.'

I want to beg you . . . to be patient toward all that is unsolved in your heart and to try to love the *question themselves* like locked rooms and like books that are written in a very foreign tongue. Do not now seek the answers, which cannot be given you because you would not be able to live them. And the point is, to live everything. *Live* the questions now. Perhaps you will then gradually, without noticing it, live along some distant day into the answer.

Rainer Maria Rilke, *Letters to a Young Poet*

2

A journey inward to be taken

We ask to know the will of God without guessing that his will is written into our very beings.

Elizabeth O'Connor

Abraham Maslow reckoned that 'the average, normal, well-adjusted person often has not the slightest idea of what he is, of what he wants, of what his own opinions are.' That may be putting it a bit strongly, but in the deeper aspects of life it is regrettably true. At this point in the life of the industrialized nations people are exceptionally out of touch with the inner springs of their nature.

An important factor that has led to this state of affairs is the change in the nature of work in the last two centuries. André Gorz writes:

> Work has not always existed in the way it is currently understood ... It means [now] an activity carried out: for someone else; in return for a wage; according to forms and time schedules laid down by the person paying the wage; and for a purpose not chosen by the worker ... The terms 'work' and 'job' have become interchangeable; work is no longer something that one *does*, but something one *has*. One 'looks for work' and 'finds work' just as one 'looks for' and 'finds' a job
> André Gorz, *Farewell to the Working Class* (Pluto 1980)

He points to the fact that for most people work has become more heteronomous (i.e. directed by others, the opposite of autonomous) than it has ever been.

Before the industrial revolution agriculture was the dominant working activity. You with your family worked your patch, or the patch allotted or rented to you. At some seasons of the year there was not enough to do on the land, and some would engage in the cottage industries, spinning, weaving, dyeing, smithing, carpentry, milling, etc. Some families would regard these activities as their main focus of work. But from late June to late September during the crisis of harvest time, 'everywhere everyone was also a worker on the land' (Peter Laslett, *The World We Have Lost*, Methuen 1965). The main reason for work was subsistence, the main focus of heteronomy was the weather. You worked all the hours of fine weather at harvest time, not because of a directive from the company's headquarters in Chicago, but because the survival of your village directly depended on it. It was only too clear what you had to do and why you had to do it.

The industrial revolution changed that for most people. For generations now workers have not been required to understand or participate in decisions about what they do, or the way they are to do it, or whether they are to have the opportunity of doing it at all. In fact they have been positively prevented from having influence in these matters. This trend has gone on for so long and gone so far that it is not surprising that we have what the Right calls 'the dependency culture'. Dispensable cogs do not quickly change into self-motivating people. But of course the current revolution in the nature of work cruelly requires that most of us will have to, and in ways for which we are ill prepared, either as individuals or as a body politic.

This change has affected our attitudes far beyond the world of paid work. It has given a much more heteronomous feel to life and reduced our expectation of self-determination in other aspects of our existence. Even outside working hours where our activities are not literally directed by others, we feel an obligation to do what we think others expect of us. That is of course a human tendency anyway, and not entirely to be regretted, since it is one of the glues that bind us together. But when pushed too far, as by the change I have described, it crushes people's initiative and creativity.

I find this change in society deeply affects the way people hear me when I talk or write about personal calling. Almost always they expect their search for their personal calling to be fulfilled by finding a ready-made niche which fits them like a glove. In the end that is a fantasy, and an evasion of the inner work that has to be done. Personal calling and the ready-made niche are a contradiction. *For a genuine personal calling there are no ready-made niches.* If there is ever to be a niche, it will be one you have made yourself. In the same way, if your particular personal calling consists not just in *what* you do but in the *way* that you do it (e.g. in your job), in so far as it is your personal calling it will not be enshrined in the job specification. In fact it is likely, at least in some respects, to be at odds with the job spec. And whether you get away with it or not will depend on how much freedom your job allows you. There is of course nothing wrong with job specifications and contracts of employment which require work to be done on other people's terms. That is an essential part of life. It is when it becomes the whole of life that the damage is done and we grow deaf even to the possibility of personal calling.

It might be as well to digress for a moment at this point to deal with a possible problem. What I am recommending may sound to some altogether too individualistic. After all, you may say, most constructive change in society is achieved not by individuals, but by people working together. There is much truth in that, but I believe that both individual initiative and co-operative effort are needed. The exercise of personal calling may look individualistic: but it is nothing if not a contribution to the common good. When our actions spring from our depths, they spring from a common humanity and become a gift to the common weal. It is when our motivation is more superficial and ego-propelled that it becomes destructive of common life. The political dogma of the 1980s gave a bad name to personal initiative by making it sound as though it were solely about making money. That is the opposite of what I am talking about (see, for example, the quotation from Elizabeth O'Connor on p. 24). The 'freedom' to make your pile has nothing to do with genuine personal freedom. To persuade people otherwise is to gull them into another kind of prison. Putting the word 'freedom' over the door is like putting the motto *Arbeit macht frei* (work makes you free) over the gates of Auschwitz.

In being open to your personal calling from God, then, there is a journey inwards to be undertaken, a journey of discovery. 'Journey' is not too big a word for it, since for most of us it requires an enormous change of attitude. For our purpose now we are concerned with the first stage of this journey: beginning to give attention to your inner life, to your own nature and feelings and perceptions and intuitions.

You may at times be tempted to think that this is selfish, or even morbid. If so, know that unwillingness to make this journey will deprive others of the gift that you will in time become for them by making it. Remember too that it will take time. The path to flowering and fruitfulness is for many of us a long and circuitous one.

Before the tree can flower, roots have to be put down deep into dark earth. In a world which expects instant results, there may not be anything to show for it for a long time.

Two things to do

- Think of a person, or a book, or an event, that has been an important influence on your development, or that has helped you to value or appreciate yourself. Take a couple of minutes to draw a rough picture to symbolize this. You may need to take a little time first to become quiet and still, perhaps with your eyes closed, to allow a suitable image or symbol to take shape in your mind. You do not need to be an artist for this kind of drawing. It is more like doodling. Stick figures will do. Drawing is a way of getting beyond words. Words *can* be a barrier to relatedness, both to others and to yourself.

- Do you dream at night? If you remember a dream on waking, write it down. Use the present tense: e.g. 'I am walking along an unfamiliar street . . .'. This helps to avoid holding the dream at arm's length. I am not suggesting you try and interpret your dreams (most of us need sensitive and skilled help to do that); rather that you allow them houseroom, instead of ignoring them or ridiculing them. They are a natural part of your inner life. Befriending your dreams is a way of befriending yourself.

———◆———

Thomas Merton said, toward the end of his life, 'If you are going to be yourself, you are not going to fit anybody else's mystique.'... Before you could be yourself, however, Merton felt you had to take the time to become yourself, to face yourself in your fundamental reality, and to peel away the accretions of mediocre or false values imposed by society, ambition and self-interest. Only then, as the overflow of such contemplation could you find your truth and your reality.

J. H. Griffin, *Thomas Merton: The Hermitage Years*
(Burns & Oates 1993)

I think all those barriers that people put up to protect themselves, the restrictions they put on their kids, are to save face. It's saying to the public, 'Hey look, we're trying our best to fit in.' I had that drummed into me as a kid, and one of the reasons I wanted to be in show business is because I had this thing of, 'Oh well, I've got to fit in and people have got to like me and I've got to aim to please.' It's only now I'm realizing that the only way to do anything well is to actually please yourself and to go with your gut instead of relying on other people. You can't live your life by committee – you've got to go with your own intuition.

Lenny Henry, comedian

And as I stood, small and lost, in the centre of that big stage, the gaping, empty chasm of the auditorium stretching out threateningly before me, I was suddenly hit by the realization that some people base their entire lives on applause from that gaping chasm.

Etty: A Diary 1941–43

If people don't recognise me, I don't exist any more.

Michel Blanc, film actor

When our life ceases to be inward and private, conversation degenerates into mere gossip. We rarely meet a man who can tell us any news which he has not read in a newspaper, or been told by his neighbor; and, for the most part, the only difference between us and our fellow is that he has seen the newspaper, or been out to tea, and we have not. In proportion as our inward life fails, we go more constantly and desperately to the post office. You may depend on it, that the poor fellow who walks away with the greatest number of letters proud of his extensive correspondence has not heard from himself this long while.

Henry David Thoreau, *Walden and Other Writings*
(Modern Library 1937)

Outside motivation is not worthy of the work we do. It separates us from our work and alienates us from our inner self. That way lies spiritual and personal death. When we work in that fashion our work is dead work.

> Those deeds which do not flow from within your inner self are all dead before God. Those are the deeds which were engendered by causes outside of yourself, because they did not proceed from life. That is why they are dead, because only that is alive which has motion within itself. Consequently, for a person's deeds to be alive, they have to come from within, not from something alien and outside himself. (Meister Eckhart)

One reason why outside-oriented works alienate us is that they are born of compulsion and not compassion or creativity, the way the creative Word gives birth.

Matthew Fox, *Breakthrough: Meister Eckhart's Creation Spirituality*
(Doubleday 1980)

Everyone speaks of living the unconscious, of the Self, of God, of inner wisdom, of following yourself and all that stuff. But when it comes down to it, we just don't trust ourselves or our perceptions enough, and do not really follow our own processes. We do not value what we see, hear, feel, how we move, relate or experience the world. No wonder so many people always feel criticized or unloved! They hate their own perceptions, and thus do not follow themselves. They cannot follow their own individual processes, but instead program themselves until they can't stand it any more.

Arnold and Amy Mindell, *Riding the Horse Backwards* (Penguin 1992)

To know yourself is the most arduous task that you can set yourself. You can go to the moon, you can do everything in life, but if you don't know yourself, you will be empty, dull, stupid. Though you may function as a prime minister or a first class engineer or a marvellous technician, you are merely functioning mechanically. So feel the importance, the seriousness of knowing yourself – not what people have said about you, whether you are the supreme self or the little self. Wipe away all the things that people have said, and observe your own minds and your own hearts, and from there function.

Krishnamurti, *On Freedom* (Gollancz 1992)

I chose to ask questions and not accept ready made answers. We discover our own answers if we have the will to do so; and if we are not afraid of the confrontation with ourselves that such a journey might entail.

Brian Keenan, *An Evil Cradling* (Arrow 1993)

It is a slow and painful process, this striving after true inner freedom. Growing more and more certain that there is no help or assurance or refuge in others. That the others are just as uncertain and weak and helpless as you are. You are always thrown back on to your own resources. There is nothing else. The rest is make-believe. But that fact has to be recognized over and over again. Especially since you are a woman. For woman always longs to lose herself in another. But that too is a fiction, albeit a beautiful one.

Etty: A Diary 1941–43

The child so easy to mold, the adolescent so anxious to conform, becomes the adult shaped from without instead of
from within. In whatever way it happens, the person who has
lost his true self has a hunger in him. It may be expressed in
apathy or in industry. He may try to satisfy it with a job he
works at fourteen hours a day, or a family that is 'everything'
to him, or success that is worth all striving, or the acquisition
of things, of which there is no end of wanting. But there is
nothing to fill the emptiness of the one who is not following
the way of his or her own inner being . . .

Sometimes the artist . . . becomes a critic of the work of
others as he grows afraid. It is as though the other were his
competitor, or could be, and he has forgotten the mysterious
uniting of elements that happens in himself to produce a
work. Either this, or he paints in the way of most people,
using only observations and techniques and skill. It may, as
with the writer, be a very good work, pleasing to the eye, but
it is not creative in the profound sense. It has not come from
the deep center of himself, where forces within him unite,
and something happens which is through him and of him,
but which even he cannot cause to happen again. The artist
who is operating on the more surface level has reason for his
fear. He has many competitors, and they may seek to occupy
his place, for after all he is not in his real place, which means
that he can be displaced. He is not even in the place of
another person, since it is not possible to take a place that
truly belongs to another.

No, the place where he is does not belong to any one. One
holds it, and then another. It is won by the usual means of
aggression, or industry, or cunning, or deceit, or skill, or
knowledge, and in these ways it can be lost. This is common
practice and there is nothing to be said about the wrong or
the right of it. This is not what we are discussing, but the fact
that there is another way – one that belongs to an entirely
different order of things, whose governing laws are different.
The place a person finds under these other laws is really their
own, and when they have found it they are not afraid, because
there has grown up in them the knowledge that it cannot be

taken away. That person is in the place that was prepared for them when the foundations of their life were laid.

The artist has been used as an example here, but only to illustrate the general plight. Each of us is the artist of his or her own life.

Elizabeth O'Connor, *Journey Inward, Journey Outward*
(my italics), adapted

The inner self is a dark room in two senses; it is obscure, hidden, unknown; it is also like a photographic darkroom where images are developed, where things are brought to light.

Alan Bennett, playwright, in a radio broadcast

Everything is gestation and then bringing forth. To let each impression and each germ of a feeling come to completion wholly in itself, in the dark, in the inexpressible, the unconscious, beyond the reach of one's own intelligence, and await with deep humility and patience the birth-hour of a new clarity.

Rainer Maria Rilke, *Letters To a Young Poet*

I am beginning to hear the lessons which whisper in my blood.

Hermann Hesse, *Demian* (tr. W. J. Strachan, Picador 1995)

My brother, do you want to go apart and be alone? Do you want to seek the way to yourself? Pause just a moment and listen to me.

'He who seeks may easily get lost himself. It is a crime to go apart and be alone' – thus speaks the herd.

The voice of the herd will still ring within you.

Friedrich Nietzsche, Thus Spoke Zarathustra (Penguin 1961)

When we discourage persons from being on an inward journey of self-discovery, we keep them from coming into possession of their own souls, keep them from finding the eternal city, keep them from being authentic persons who use their gifts and personality to mediate God's peace and God's love. He or she who tries to keep another from the pilgrim path of self-discovery is doing the devil's work, and a lot of frightened persons are about that work.

Elizabeth O'Connor Letters to Scattered Pilgrims (Harper & Row 1979)

The journey that the artist makes in turning inward to listen to and trust his or her images is a communal journey... The artist who is truly birthing from the depths of the inside is birthing from the depths of commonality.

Matthew Fox, Breakthrough (Doubleday 1980)

Give me a candle of the Spirit, O God, as I go down into the deeps of my being. Show me the hidden things, the creatures of my dreams, the storehouse of forgotten memories and hurts. Take me down to the spring of my life, and tell me my nature and my name. Give me freedom to grow, so that I may become that self, the seed of which you planted in me at my making. Out of the deeps I cry to you, O God.

George Appleton, One Man's Prayers (SPCK 1976),
adapted by Jim Cotter

3

The cost

It is narrow gate and a hard road that leads to life.

The Gospel of Matthew

A favourite theme in human story-telling is the journey through many vicissitudes and perils in search of some prized object or person or place. Such is the quest of the prince in this chapter (p. 32). There are many symbolic features in that story. For our purpose, one of the most important is the parrot-shooting episode. The parrot represents the spirit of imitation. Unless we succeed in avoiding the trap of assuming we have to model ourselves on someone else's life and activity, however admirable they may be, we shall be turned to stone: we shall atrophy and dry up. Notice also the three shots he has, which well illustrate the paradox of personal calling. On the one hand we need to put all we have got into it, every ounce of effort, care, diligence, generous-heartedness, and willingness to take risks. But in the end it is God's work: and through it other people will be brought to life. Other features to notice are the mirror (a symbol of the importance of self-knowledge), and the long and painful wandering in the desert. If by any chance your motto is 'anything for a quiet life', it might be as well to consign this book to the bin at this point!

There are really two overlapping themes in this chapter. One concerns the cost of the journey *towards* the discovery of your personal calling. The other is about the cost of actually responding to God's call to you when it has become clear. The Chaim Potok quotation (p. 35) beautifully illustrates the latter and expresses the sense of fraud and dishonesty when you hang back from the fullness of what you know you should be doing. Do not let the fact that it is about painting mislead you. The work of an artist stands for any 'called' activity. We are all to be the artists of what we do. Whenever we withhold ourselves, or rest content with repeating ourselves, or

27

shirk the risk of doing what we are for, we shall be haunted – and rightly so – by a feeling of integrity betrayed.

In the first excerpt in this chapter Jesus says we are to renounce ourselves and take up our cross and follow him. All three of these injunctions have been widely misunderstood. Renouncing ourselves does not mean becoming doormats or non-persons, at least not in one bound! Elisabeth Kübler-Ross (p. 30) unpacks something of what it might truly involve. If *after that* we are accounted non-persons (which may well happen in our world of topsy-turvy values), that is not the same as shirking the growth process in the first place. The cross has sometimes been presented as though it were an end in itself, as though Christianity were a way of death rather than the way to life. But the cross is not something you choose or select or aim for. It describes the kind of thing that can happen to you if you respond to God's personal calling to you (like it did to Jesus). It points also to the painful aspects of your journey to a more full-blooded and fruitful life. If you like, the cross is a symbol of the cost of truly living. As for Jesus' call to follow him, this does not mean he wants us to imitate him in some literal, parrot-like way, as we shall see in chapter 6.

A question to ponder

- Your journey to fulfilment and fruitfulness will require of you some letting go, some stripping, some suffering even. What might you have to let go of to travel this road?

———— ✦ ————

Then Jesus told his disciples, 'If any want to become my followers, let them deny themselves and take up their cross and follow me. For those who want to save their life will lose it, and those who lose their life for my sake will find it. For what will it profit them if they gain the whole world but forfeit their life? Or what will they give in return for their life?'

Matthew 16.24–6 (NRSV)

The old lie about self-denial still keeps spooking around in the psyches of many Christians. It says that Christianity is about squashing your feelings, doing your duty and soldiering on regardless. It leads eventually to chronic exhaustion, cynicism, depression, or drink – or all four. That is a well-recognized condition known as burnout, grey-faced and driven, and when we get into that, no matter how virtuous or good the work itself may be, it will not convey good news to anyone. To use St Paul's words, it is to be under the law.

Do not misunderstand me. There is nothing wrong with self-denial; but we do need to exercise some care in defining what is meant by the first of those two words. I am at some pains in this book to explain that God calls you to discover your true self, that greater self that you could become, and to let it flower generously in some specific activity at his gracious invitation. To deny yourself does *not* mean nipping this process in the bud. But allowing this flowering may mean foregoing popularity, or status, or your good name, or money, or power, or security; the kind of things that advertisers try to persuade us are essential. In other words, it *will* mean denying the self that runs after or clings to these things; that part of our nature that we call our ego *will* need to be subdued and crushed – a painful process, very painful, but not a destructive one. It is the grain of wheat falling to the ground and dying (John 12.24), that it may bear a rich harvest. To the extent that our ego is not subjugated it will blight both the flowering and the fruitfulness.

Francis Dewar

You must give up everything in order to gain everything. What must you give up? All that is not truly you; all that you have chosen without choosing and value without evaluating, accepting because of someone else's extrinsic judgment, rather than your own; all your self-doubt that keeps you from trusting and loving yourself or other human beings. What will you gain? Only your own, true self; a self who is at peace, who is able to truly love and be loved, and who understands who and what [s]he is meant for. But you can be yourself only if you are no one else. You must give up 'their' approval, whoever *they* are, and look to yourself for evaluation of success and failure, in terms of your *own* level of aspiration that is consistent with *your* values. Nothing is simpler and nothing is more difficult.

Elisabeth Kübler-Ross, *Death: The Final Stage of Growth*
(Prentice-Hall 1975)

Gospel people don't need to hang on to anything. For them, the ego is out of the way. They'll make a difference in the world precisely because they don't need to. They don't need to be first, they don't need to be important, they don't need to be number one. They don't need to be rich, secure, popular, so they can do what God has told them to do. They can be obedient, God can move through them with power. That's why spirituality is always about letting go.

Richard Rohr, *Radical Grace* (St Anthony Messenger Press 1993)

'The kingdom of heaven is like treasure hidden in a field which someone has found; he hides it again, goes off happy, sells everything he owns and buys the field.

'Again, the kingdom of heaven is like a merchant looking for fine pearls; when he finds one of great value he goes and sells everything he owns and buys it.'

Matthew 13.44–6

There is an inner reality within each of us which is like a great treasure lying hidden in the field of our soul waiting to be discovered. When someone finds this inner treasure, and recognizes its value, he happily gives up all other goals and ambitions in order to make it real in his life.

Now let us compare this with the second parable . . .

At first glance it looks as if this parable duplicates the parable of the treasure. But, as Fritz Kunkel has pointed out, in the first parable the kingdom is a treasure which *we* search for and find; in the second parable the kingdom is likened to a merchant who is searching for things of value. In this case *we* are the pearls, found by the kingdom of God.

John Sanford, *The Kingdom Within* (J. B. Lippincott 1970)

The important thing is not the finding, it is the seeking, it is the devotion with which one spins the wheel of prayer and scripture, discovering the truth little by little. If this machine gave you the truth immediately, you would not recognize it, because your heart would not have been purified by a long quest.

Umberto Eco, quoted by Sr Wendy Beckett, *Art and the Sacred* (Rider 1992)

A great and noble prince receives orders from his king to investigate the mysterious Bath of Badgerd. When he approaches it, having gone through many dangerous adventures, he hears that nobody ever returned from it: but he insists on going on. He is received at a round building by a barber with a mirror who leads him into the bath; but as soon as the prince enters the water, a thunderous noise breaks out, it gets completely dark, the barber disappears, and slowly the water begins to rise.

The prince swims desperately round until the water finally reaches the top of the round cupola, which forms the roof of the bath. Now he fears he is lost, but he says a prayer and grabs the centre-stone of the cupola. Again a thunderous noise, everything changes, and he stands alone in a desert.

After long and painful wandering, he comes to a beautiful garden in the middle of which is a circle of stone statues. In the centre of the statues, he sees a parrot in its cage, and a voice from above says to him: 'O hero, you probably will not escape alive from this bath. Once Gayomart, the First Man, found an enormous diamond that shone more brightly than sun and moon. He decided to hide it where no one could find it, and therefore he built this magical bath in order to protect it. The parrot that you see here forms part of the magic. At its feet lie a golden bow and arrow on a golden chain, and with them you may try three times to shoot the parrot. If you hit him the curse will be lifted; if not, you will be petrified, as were all these other people.'

The prince tries once, and fails. His legs turn to stone. He shoots a second time and misses, and is petrified up to his chest. The third time he just shuts his eyes, exclaiming 'God is great,' shoots blindly, and this time hits the parrot. An outbreak of thunder, clouds of dust! When all this has subsided, in place of the parrot is an enormous, beautiful diamond, and all the statues have come to life again. The people thank him for their redemption.

An Iranian fairy-tale

Enter by the narrow gate, since the road that leads to perdition is wide and spacious, and many take it; but it is a narrow gate and a hard road that leads to life, and only a few find it.

Matthew 7.13–14

Are we to believe, then, that there is no way to step out of the crowd? Not so. While it is true that all things conspire against it, God conspires for it. There comes an event, or a flash of insight, or a demanding ache. There comes a person who is in the crowd, but not of it. These are moments God uses to put in the heart and the mouth the question, 'Is there another way?' When that question is asked, one can begin to hear about the inward journey, or the 'narrow gate'. But from learning that there are two ways – one that leads to death and one to life – it does not follow that we enter by the narrow gate. The facts about that gate are starkly simple.

> One, it leads to life, but
> Two, it is a hard way, and
> Three, few find it.

For those who would be on the inward journey, these are three facts to ponder at the beginning and end of each day. We must cling to the first against temptations, and false prophets, and glittering goals. We must hold to the second lest we be too easily turned aside or corrupted by the illusion that something can be had for nothing. It is part of our sickness that we go after the high prize with so little understanding of the cost and so poorly equipped to meet and withstand the armies that will do battle against us. We do not ask for courage, because we do not know we have need of it. We are given over into the hands of the enemy without having discerned his shape on the horizon.

The persons who would step out of the crowd and follow their own destiny, must keep before them the knowledge that the way is hard. But even if they are aware of this, they are still in danger. They must remember, also, that few find it. It will grow easy for them to imagine that they are on the way when they are not. This is where the religious lose out on the Kingdom. They assume that because they are aware of the two ways, and because they have chosen the second, they are on it. This is to fall comfortably into the sleep of the crowd again. It may well be a 'religious' crowd, but it is nonetheless a crowd.

Elizabeth O'Connor, *Journey Inward, Journey Outward*, adapted

Michelangelo was sweating as he manoeuvred a large rock down the street. An onlooker standing idly at a doorway asked why on earth he was expending so much effort shifting a lump of stone. 'Because', came the reply, 'there is an angel in there that wants to walk free.'

I looked a very long time at the painting and knew it was incomplete. It was a good painting but it was incomplete. The telephone poles were only distant reminders of the brutal reality of a crucifix. The painting did not say fully what I had wanted to say; it did not reflect fully the anguish and torment I had wanted to put into it. Within myself, a warning voice spoke soundlessly of fraud.

I had brought something incomplete into the world. Now I felt its incompleteness. 'Can you understand what it means for something to be incomplete?' my mother had once asked me. I understood, I understood.

I turned away from the painting and walked to the yeshiva. I had supper and prayed the evening service. I returned to the apartment. Children played on the cobblestone street below my window. I stared at the painting and felt cold with dread. Then I went to bed and lay awake in the darkness, listening to the sounds of the street through my open window: a quarrel, a distant cough, a passing car, the cry of a child – all of it filtered through my feeling of cold dread. I slept very little. In the morning, I woke and prayed and knew what had to be done.

Yes, I could have decided not to do it. Who would have known? Would it have made a difference to anyone in the world that I had felt a sense of incompleteness about a painting? Who would have cared about my silent cry of fraud? Only Jacob Kahn, and perhaps one or two others, might have sensed its incompleteness. And even they could never have known how incomplete it truly was, for by itself it was a good painting. Only I would have known.

But it would have made me a whore to leave it incomplete. It would have made it easier to leave future work incomplete. It would have made it more and more difficult to draw upon that additional aching surge of effort that is always the difference between integrity and deceit in a created work. I would not be the whore to my own existence. Can you understand that? I would not be the whore to my own existence.

Chaim Potok, *My Name is Asher Lev* (Penguin 1973)

Deep in the sea are riches beyond compare.
But if you seek safety, it is on the shore.

Saadi of Shiraz

Forgive us, O Lord, we acknowledge ourselves as type
    of the common man.
Of the men and women who shut the door and sit
    by the fire;
Who fear the blessing of God, the loneliness of the
    night of God, the surrender required, the
    deprivation inflicted;
Who fear the injustice of men less than the justice
    of God;
Who fear the hand at the window, the fire in the thatch,
    the fist in the tavern, the push into the canal,
Less than we fear the love of God.
We acknowledge our trespass, our weakness, our fault.

T. S. Eliot, 'Murder in the Cathedral', The Complete Poems and
Plays of T. S. Eliot (Faber & Faber 1969)

4

Be still and know

The secret is this: to grow quiet and listen.

Alan McGlashan

As I write this it is summer and the city centre is full of people on holiday. As they stand camera in hand in the market place or by the cathedral I sometimes wonder how many of them are really *seeing* what they are photographing, and how many are already, even as they stand there, imagining how the snaps will look in the photo album at home, or how their friends will react to the video they are filming. For, to see the cathedral it is necessary to be present to it, to be there with all your senses sharpened, not 'miles away' in your living room. The camera *can* be an aid to seeing; often it is a substitute for it.

The theme of this section is receptiveness and openness to reality. I only really see, or hear, or feel, in so far as I am, from moment to moment, aware and awake and open to what is. The pieces by Krishnamurti and Frederick Franck make abundantly clear the difference between seeing and not seeing. It is so simple. Why then do so few of us open our eyes?

Some years ago we lived in a house built on the side of a hill with a panoramic view. Behind and slightly above us was a house with a large upstairs room with a bay window which had an even better view. But the occupants used it as a junk room. Occasionally I would notice the wife standing there ironing, with her back to the window!

Recently I revisited the church in the village where I lived for two or three years in the 1950s. I was astonished to find that from the churchyard you could see for miles over rolling countryside. When I lived there I do not remember ever noticing the view.

My guess is that how much we see is in inverse proportion to the amount of undischarged distress of one kind or another that we carry about with us, feelings like fear, grief or anger, the effect of some of the things that happen to us, especially in our earliest years. Although we may not be directly aware of them, these buried feelings seem to siphon off our attention and dull our sensitivity to the people and things around us. I think this is one reason why we do not see, and most of us need some help in dealing with this barrier to awareness (see chapter 7).

Another reason why we do not see is our tendency to put names to things, to label them, instead of simply opening our awareness to them. Maybe this is because at school, generally speaking, it is our intellects that are developed, while our senses tend to be depreciated. I should point out here that though I am talking mainly of seeing, what I am recommending is just as important for a blind person. In other words, seeing stands for awareness of all kinds.

Why is awareness and openness to reality so important a factor in the discernment of personal calling? To hear a call from God requires deep and genuine openness in three ways:

* first, to the world as it is and to people as they are;
* second, to myself as I am, with my leanings and longings, my gifts and wounds and possibilities;
* third, to the tiny hints and nudgings of God who invites me to put the second in some way or other at the service of the first.

Without openness and awareness there can be no seeing or listening or realistic responding. There will only be:

* my assumptions about what people's needs are;
* my blinkered notions of what my capabilities are;
* my preconceived ideas of what God wants of me.

But that is not all. Very often the labelling process itself is a major obstacle to a person's exploration of what God is inviting them to offer. People only search among the labels, as it were. They do not really open their minds and hearts to their real possibilities. Your particular personal calling will not have a label. Only standardized activities have labels. For example, in casual conversation I dread being asked 'By the way, what do you do?' I do not have a job as such, and no label would describe what I do. Sometimes I duck the question, 'It's too difficult to explain,' I say, 'that's why I write books about it!' I suspect that if you can describe your personal calling adequately in one sentence, it is not yet your *personal* calling – just a stepping stone on the way to it, perhaps.

So there is the need for this openness, this awareness, as though there were a deep silence at the very centre of you, an ability to hear and receive the slightest sound without distorting it. There *is* a deep silence at the centre of each of us, but most of us are far too activist and cluttered and busy to know it. Though I do think many people dimly sense it. The amazing popularity of records of plainsong or of the music of people like Gorecki bear testimony to this. It is music that does not really go anywhere. It is repetitive, like a mantra, which is after all one of the traditional routes to inner silence. But inner silence is not only necessary for awareness of God. It is the prerequisite also for being present to ourselves and to one another.

Something to do

- My sister was a musician. I remember at one stage she was told by her teacher that before starting to play she should sit quietly for several minutes just listening and sharpening her ears. Try it. You do not have to be musical. Just close your eyes and be aware of all the sounds there are. Resist the temptation to label them 'car', 'blackbird', 'clock'. Be aware of all the detail of the humming, or clattering, or whirring. Listen to the rise and fall of the fluting and piping, the changing texture of each note. Notice the inner detail of each tick. Once you really open your ears, you will find it impossible to describe in words what you hear.
- Then open your eyes and begin to look at whatever is in your field of view. Choose an object to look at as though you were going to draw it. Notice its shapes and textures, its light and dark, its shifting shades of colour. Be aware of more and more detail as you begin actually to see this object.
- Later you could begin to walk slowly, making each movement deliberately, being aware as you do so of all the dozens of little sensations involved in the simple act of putting one foot in front of the other.

Much of our lack of awareness is simply habit. A good way to get out of this habitual insensitivity is to practise these simple awareness exercises whenever you have an opportunity. But you will find it easier if there are spaces in your day. If you are distracted and rushed most of the time, it will be more difficult – and even more important.

◆

Everyone needs enough silence and solitude in their lives to enable that deep inner voice of their own true self to be heard at least occasionally. When that inner voice is not heard, when we cannot attain to the spiritual peace that comes from being perfectly at one with our own true selves, our lives are always miserable and exhausting. For no-one can go on happily for long unless they are in contact with the springs of spiritual life which are hidden in the depths of their own soul. If we are constantly exiled from our own home, locked out of our own spiritual solitude, we cease to be true people. We no longer live as human beings. We are not even healthy animals. We become... automatons, living without joy because we have lost all spontaneity. We are no longer moved from within, but only from outside ourselves. We no longer make decisions for ourselves, we let them be made for us. We no longer act upon the outside world, but let it act upon us. We are propelled through life by a series of collisions with outside forces. Ours is no longer the life of a human being, but the existence of a sentient billiard ball, a being without purpose and without any deeply valid response to reality.

Thomas Merton, *The Silent Life* (Sheldon Press 1975), adapted

It seems that the great humanizers of our lifetime have all arrived at these fundamental truths clarified for us in Thomas Merton's life and writings: the tremendous necessity of first *being* and then *doing*; and the impossibility of this without the interior freedom to transcend ourselves. Yet every single such person has been considered highly controversial and has in some way been martyred for the love of fellow human beings. The bewilderment comes from wondering what is controversial in any of this.

J. H. Griffin, *Thomas Merton: The Hermitage Years*

If you are wise, you will become a reservoir rather than a canal. A canal distributes its water as fast as it receives it; but a reservoir is content to wait until it is filled before overflowing, and thus without loss to itself, it communicates its superabundant water to others... In the Church of the present day, we have many canals but few reservoirs.

Bernard of Clairvaux (1090–1153)

For thus said the Lord GOD, the Holy One of Israel,
 'In returning and rest you shall be saved:
in quietness and in trust shall be your strength.'

Isaiah 30.15 (RSV)

In the course of their journey [Jesus] came to the village, and
a woman named Martha welcomed him into her house. She
had a sister called Mary, who sat down at the Lord's feet and
listened to him speaking. Now Martha who was distracted
with all the serving said, 'Lord, do you not care that my
sister is leaving me to do the serving all by myself? Please tell
her to help me.' But the Lord answered: 'Martha, Martha,' he
said, 'you worry and fret about so many things, and yet few
are needed, indeed only one. It is Mary who has chosen the
better part; it is not to be taken from her.'

Luke 10.38–42

The artist is always the contemplative – the one who sees what is there. The uninhibited three-year-old, stopping with enthralled gaze to watch an insect, or some activity in the street, is also a contemplative. If we could recover that lost capacity to look, which we all once had, we might be able to penetrate to the heart of matters.

Elizabeth O'Connor, *Cry Pain, Cry Hope*

You know, when you look at a sunset or a lovely face or a beautiful leaf or a flower, when you actually see it, then there is space between you and that flower and that beauty and that loveliness, or between you and the misery and the squalor you see. There is space; you have not created it, it is there. You cannot do anything to make that space wide or narrow, it is there. But we refuse to look through that space simply, quietly, persistently. Through that space we project our opinions, our ideas, our conclusions, our formulas, and therefore there is no space. That space is covered over with yesterdays, with the memories, with the experiences of yesterday; therefore we never see, we never listen, we are never quiet.

Krishnamurti, *On Freedom*

Whenever I saw a beautiful flower, what I longed to do with it was press it to my heart, or eat it all up. It was more difficult with a piece of beautiful scenery, but the feeling was the same. I was too sensual, I might almost write too greedy. I yearned physically for all I thought was beautiful, wanted to own it . . .

It all suddenly changed, God alone knows by what inner process, but it is different now. I realized it only this morning, when I recalled my short walk round the Skating Club a few nights ago. It was dusk, soft hues in the sky, mysterious silhouettes of houses, trees alive with the light through the tracery of their branches, in short, enchanting. And then I knew precisely how I had felt in the past. Then all that beauty would have gone like a stab to my heart and I would not have known what to do with the pain. Then I would have felt the need to write, to compose verses, but the words would still have refused to come. I would have felt utterly miserable, wallowed in the pain and exhausted myself as a result . . .

But that night, only just gone, I reacted quite differently. I felt that God's world was beautiful despite everything, but its beauty now filled me with joy. I was just as deeply moved by that mysterious, still landscape in the dusk as I might have been before, but somehow I no longer wanted to own it. I went home invigorated and got back to work.

Etty: A Diary 1941–43

Please watch yourself. See how insensitive your mind has become. When you have a feeling of pleasure or pain, of a spontaneous joy of something, the moment you feel it there is an immediate response to it by naming it; you name it instantly. Please follow this, observe it in yourself. Because if you don't follow all this, when I talk about freedom, it will mean nothing to you. I am talking about a mind that does not name. When you have a feeling, you name it instantly, you give it a name. The very process of naming it is the state of non-observation. You name it in order to fix it as an experience in your memory, and then, the next day, that memory, which has become mechanical, wants it repeated. Therefore when you look at the sunset the next day, it is no longer the thing that you looked at spontaneously, the first day. So the naming process of any feeling, in any observation, prevents you from looking.

Krishnamurti, *On Freedom*

People in the car rave about the landscape: 'Oh, how lovely …' As soon as I sit down in that landscape with my pen, it is no longer 'Oh, how lovely…' It simply *is*, simple in its intricate complexity.

Frederick Franck, *The Zen of Seeing* (Vintage Books 1973)

Everyone thinks he knows what a lettuce looks like. But start to draw one and you realise the anomaly of having lived with lettuces all your life but never having seen one . . .

What applies to lettuces, applies equally to the all-too-familiar faces of husbands . . . wives . . .

I have learned that what I have not drawn I have never really seen.

Frederick Franck, *The Zen of Seeing*

Delight is a secret. And the secret is this: to grow quiet and listen; to stop thinking, stop moving, almost to stop breathing; to create an inner stillness in which, like mice in a deserted house, capacities and awarenesses too wayward and too fugitive for everyday use may delicately emerge. Oh, welcome them home! For these are the long-lost children of the human mind. Give them close and loving attention, for they are weakened by centuries of neglect. In return they will open your eyes to a new world within the known world, they will take your hand, as children do, and bring you where life is always nascent, day always dawning.

Alan McGlashan, *The Savage and Beautiful Country*
(Daimon Verlag 1988)

The ultimate purpose of emptiness, then, is to make room. Room for what? Room for God, the religious would say. But since God means so many things to different people, including nothing at all, I prefer generally to say that emptiness makes room for the Other. What is the Other? It can be virtually anything: a tale from a strange culture, the different, the unexpected, the new, the better. Most important, for community, the Other is the Stranger, the other person. We cannot even let the other person into our hearts or minds unless we empty ourselves. We can truly listen to him or truly hear her only out of emptiness.

M. Scott Peck, *The Different Drum* (Arrow Books 1990)

I think that I'll do it anyway: I'll 'turn inwards' for half-an-hour each morning before work, and listen to my inner voice. Lose myself. You could also call it meditation. I am still a bit wary of that word. But anyway, why not? A quiet half-hour within yourself . . .

But it's not so simple, that sort of 'quiet hour'. It has to be learnt. A lot of unimportant inner litter and bits and pieces have to be swept out first. Even a small head can be piled high inside with irrelevant distractions. True, there may be edifying emotions and thoughts, too, but the clutter is ever present. So let this be the aim of the meditation: to turn one's innermost being into a vast empty plain, with none of that treacherous undergrowth to impede the view. So that something of 'God' can enter you, and something of 'Love' too. Not the kind of love-de-luxe that you revel in deliciously for half an hour, taking pride in how sublime you can feel, but the love you can apply to small, everyday things.

Etty: A Diary 1941–43

Broadly speaking, this prayer strikes those who come to it as something rather unimpressive. A frequent reaction is given in the phrase, 'I am doing nothing'. There is a general sense of untidiness. Nothing seems to be happening. There are moments of more intense consolation, but they are few. In good times there is a sense of peace and contentment, a satisfaction in prayer which appears difficult to explain, since there is seemingly nothing to account for the satisfaction. In the lean years prayer is distressing because it appears such a waste of time – nothing but an unavailing effort to chase a clutter of hens out of the flower-garden, throwing stones with one hand, as it were, at pertinacious distractions, and with the other hand groping in the dark for something, or someone.

Leonard Boase, *The Prayer of Faith* (DLT 1976)

I said, 'I am naught in the world, if you do not become my companion.' He replied, 'Be naught in this world so that you clearly see my face.'

Jalaludin Rumi

Be still and know that I am God.

Psalm 46.10 (ASB)

5

Be open to the reality of God

My thoughts are not your thoughts, my ways not your ways.

Isaiah

In the past decade or two it has been fashionable, in Anglican churches at any rate, to bring the altar forward from the east end to a position not far from the front row of the congregation and have the priest face the people. We did this at the church where I was vicar in the 1970s. One man said he felt quite alarmed by it, because he felt it was bringing God too near for comfort. I sometimes wonder whether one of the functions of the Church is to keep the reality of God at a safe distance!

In this section, I shall be encouraging you to look beyond the neat orthodoxies, as we all must if we are to encounter the living God. Inevitably, as we look towards God, as through a darkened windowpane before closing the curtains, we sometimes see only the reflection of our own faces. Often, it is difficult to know whether it is our faces we are seeing or whether we are getting genuine hints of what lies behind these surface reflections. In the discernment of personal calling it is of the utmost importance that we apprehend something of the true nature of God. The world is full of people who think that what they do is the will of God! Without growing self-knowledge, true knowledge of God is impossible.

Something to reflect on

- What is your conception of God?
- How did you come to that way of thinking? By what stages?
- What people or events in your life have influenced how you think of God?

A philosopher, having made an appointment for a discussion with Nasrudin, called, but found him away from home. Infuriated, he picked up a piece of chalk and wrote 'Stupid Oaf' on Nasrudin's door.

As soon as he got home and saw this, the Mullah rushed round to the philosopher's house, 'I had forgotten', he said, 'that you were to call. I do apologise for not having been at home. Of course, I remembered the appointment as soon as I saw that you had left your name on my door.'

It is often said that atheism is terrifying, but it's not nearly as terrifying as the hard-faced tyranny of a single, omnipotent God.

Nicci Gerrard, (*Observer,* 17.12.95)

Our notion of God is mediated to us through parents, teachers and clergy. We do not come to know God directly. If our experience of parents and teachers has been of dominating people who show little affection or respect for us as persons, but value us only in so far as we conform to their expectations, then this experience is bound to affect our notion of God and will influence the way we relate to him. Our notion of God is not only inadequate; it may also be distorted.

Gerard Hughes, *God of Surprises* (DLT 1985)

An elephant belonging to a travelling exhibition had been stabled near a town where no elephant had been seen before. Four curious citizens, hearing of this hidden wonder, went to see if they could get a preview of it. When they arrived at the stable they found that there was no light. The investigation therefore had to be carried out in the dark. One, touching its trunk, thought that the creature must resemble a hosepipe; the second felt an ear and concluded it was a fan. The third, feeling a leg, could liken it only to a living pillar; and when the fourth put his hand on its back he was convinced that it was some kind of throne. None could form the complete picture; and of the part which each felt, he could only refer to it in terms of things which he already knew.

Jalaludin Rumi

Matters of spirituality are intimately bound up with context. Who you are and where you are play a quite critical part in determining the God whom you meet.

Alan Billings (1989), in a lecture in Wakefield Cathedral

I have been reading the Old Testament. I like it.

The picture it gives of you, O Lord, is not flattering: but it rings true.

It says that you are terrifying: there can be no doubt of that.

It says that you are jealous, and take revenge. Genocide means nothing to you. Wipe out all the Amalekites, man, woman and child: that is what you told King Saul to do. According to the Book of Kings.

I cannot admire this, as a Christian pacifist: but it is at least honest. God, you are not mealy-mouthed: you call a spade a spade.

You are arbitrary: you do just what you like, says the Old Testament. What you do is always good, because 'Good' is nothing but a description of what you do. You are utterly free. You make up morality. In fact, you make everything.

You are a maker, first and foremost. I like that. You made man in your own image, says the Old Testament. I like that. You intend that I should be a maker, yes?

At your peril, says the Old Testament. All right then: at my peril . . .

The great thing about you is that you are powerful and full of life. You do what you like. Nobody can tie you down, nobody can catch you in the net of a name or image. You are openended, infinite.

You are terrifying; but you are exhilarating.

Sydney Carter, *Dance in the Dark* (Fount 1980)

God is not only to be loved, but also to be feared. He fills us with evil as well as with good, otherwise he would not need to be feared; and because he wants to become man, the uniting of his antinomy must take place in man. This involves man in a new responsibility. He can no longer wriggle out of it on the plea of his littleness and nothingness, for the dark God has slipped the atom bomb and chemical weapons into his hands and given him the power to empty out the apocalyptic vials of wrath on his fellow creatures. Since he has been granted an almost godlike power, he can no longer remain blind and unconscious. He must know something of God's nature and of metaphysical processes if he is to understand himself . . .

C. G. Jung, *Answer to Job* (Ark Paperbacks 1984)

God's a rumour, if you like. Christianity, or indeed any other religion that is a religion because of fear of death or hope that there is something beyond death, does not interest me. What kind of cruel old bugger is God if it's terror that is the ruling edifice, the structure of religion – and too often, for many people, it is. Now that to me isn't religion . . .

I see God in us or with us, if I see God at all, as shreds and particles and rumours, some knowledge that we have, some feeling why we sing and dance and act, why we paint, why we love, why we make art.

Dennis Potter, playwright, in his last television interview

Last night, shortly before going to bed, I suddenly went down on my knees in the middle of this large room, between the steel chairs and the matting. Almost automatically. Forced to the ground by something stronger than myself. Some time ago I said to myself, 'I am a kneeler in training.' I was still embarrassed by this act, as intimate as gestures of love that cannot be put into words either, except by a poet. A patient once said to S., 'I sometimes have the feeling that God is right inside me, for instance when I hear the St Matthew Passion.' And S. said something like: 'At such moments you are completely at one with the creative and cosmic forces that are at work in every human being.' And these creative forces are ultimately part of God, but you need courage to put that into words.

Etty: A Diary 1941–43

Moses said, 'Show me your glory, I beg you.' And he said, 'I will let all my splendour pass in front of you, and I will pronounce before you the name Yahweh. I have compassion on whom I will, and I show pity to whom I please. You cannot see my face,' he said, 'for no one shall see me and live.' And Yahweh said, 'Here is a place beside me. You must stand on the rock, and when my glory passes by, I will put you in a cleft of the rock and shield you with my hand while I pass by. Then I will take my hand away and you shall see the back of me; but my face is not to be seen.'

Exodus 33.18–23

'Jahweh Sabaoth
Adonai, Elohim –
What shall I call you,
God, O God?'
said Moses in agony
Moses trembling
Moses under
the judgment rod.

But the Lord exploded
in glorious laughter.
'I am who I am –
have you got it? Good.
Ask a silly question
and you'll get a silly answer!'
And Moses smiled
and understood.

Simon Baynes, 'The Conversion of Moses' in A. Marriage (ed.),
New Christian Poetry (Collins Flame 1990)

For my thoughts are not your thoughts,
my ways not your ways – it is Yahweh who speaks.
Yes, the heavens are as high above earth
as my ways are above your ways,
my thoughts above your thoughts.

Isaiah 55.8–9

At times God had seemed so real and so intimately close. We talked not of a God in the Christian tradition but some force more primitive, more immediate and more vital, a presence rather than a set of beliefs. Our frankness underlined the reality of our feelings. We were both still trying to deal with the force and the weight of them. We prayed unashamedly, making no outward sign. We simply knew that each of us did pray and would on occasion remind each other to say a prayer for someone in particular among our families and lovers. In its own way our isolation had expanded the heart, not to reach out to a detached God but to find and become part of whatever 'God' might be. The energizing experience of another human being did not allow either of us to dwell too long on these matters, which were deep and unresolvable. We gave honestly of ourselves and of our experience and each received from the other with gratitude whatever was given. On occasion there would be discussions on vaguely religious themes, but they were certainly not confined by the dictates of strait-laced doctrines. We had each gone through an experience that gave us the foundations of an insight into what a humanized God might be.

Brian Keenan, *An Evil Cradling*

I went to bed early last night and from my bed I stared out through the large open window. And it was once more as if life with all its mysteries was close to me, as if I could touch it. I had the feeling that I was resting against the naked breast of life, and could feel her gentle and regular heartbeat. I felt safe and protected. And I thought: how strange. It is wartime. There are concentration camps. I can say of so many of the houses I pass: here the son has been thrown into prison, there the father has been taken hostage, and an 18-year-old boy in that house over there has been sentenced to death. And these streets and houses are all so close to my own. I know how very nervous people are, I know about the mounting human suffering. I know the persecution and oppression and despotism and the impotent fury and the terrible sadism. I know it all.

And yet – at unguarded moments, when left to myself, I

suddenly lie against the naked breast of life and her arms round me are so gentle and so protective and my own heartbeat is difficult to describe: so slow and so regular and so soft, almost muffled, but so constant, as if it would never stop.

Etty: A Diary 1941–43

I hear my Beloved.
See how he comes
leaping on the mountains,
bounding over the hills.
My Beloved is like a gazelle,
like a young stag.

See where he stands
behind our wall.
He looks in at the window,
he peers through the lattice.

My Beloved lifts up his voice,
he says to me,
'Come then, my love,
my lovely one, come.
For see, winter is past,
the rains are over and gone.
The flowers appear on the earth.
The season of glad songs has come,
the cooing of the turtledove is heard
in our land.
The fig tree is forming its first figs
and the blossoming vines give out their fragrance.
Come then, my love,
my lovely one, come.
My dove, hiding in the clefts of the rock,
in the coverts of the cliff,
show me your face,
let me hear your voice;
for your voice is sweet
and your face is beautiful.'

Song of Songs 2.8–14

That same night Jacob rose, and taking his two wives and his two slave-girls and his eleven children he crossed the ford of the Jabbok. He took them and sent them across the stream and sent all his possessions over too. And Jacob was left alone.

And there was one that wrestled with him until daybreak who, seeing that he could not master him, struck him in the socket of his hip, and Jacob's hip was dislocated as he wrestled with him. He said, 'Let me go, for day is breaking.' But Jacob answered, 'I will not let you go unless you bless me.' He then asked, 'What is your name?' 'Jacob,' he replied. He said, 'Your name shall no longer be Jacob, but Israel, because you have been strong against God, you shall prevail against men.' Jacob then made this request, 'I beg you, tell me your name,' but he replied, 'Why do you ask my name?' And he blessed him there.

Jacob named the place Peniel, 'Because I have seen God face to face,' he said, 'and I have survived.'

Genesis 32.22–30

Prayer begins at the moment when, instead of thinking of a remote God, 'He', 'The Almighty', and so forth, one can think in terms of 'Thou', when it is no longer a relationship in the third person but in the first and second persons. Take, for instance, the Book of Job, where there is a conflict. Take so many other instances in Scripture and in life, in the lives of saints and sinners, when there was tension and a violent confrontation. This is always a personal thing. There is no prayer as long as there is a cautious, distant and chilly relationship, as long as there is ceremonial between us and God, as long as we cannot speak to Him but must go through a long and complex series of words and actions. But there is a moment when, instead of all this, we pierce through and speak in the first and second person. We say 'I' and we expect Him to be 'Thou', or 'You' in the singular. Let it not be the polite, the royal 'You' but the singular and unique 'You'.

Anthony Bloom, *School for Prayer* (DLT 1970)

God ran away
when we imprisoned her
and put her in a box
named church.
God would have none
of our labels and
our limitations
and she said,
'I will escape and plant myself
in simpler soil
where those who see, will see,
and those who hear, will hear.
I will become a God – believable,
because I am free,
and go where I will.
My goodness will be found
in my freedom and
that freedom I offer to all –
regardless of colour, sex, or status,
regardless of power or money.

Ah, I am God
because I am free
and all those who would be free
will find me,
roaming, wandering, singing.
Come, walk with me –
come, dance with me!
I created you to sing – to dance,
to love . . .'

If you cannot sing,
nor dance, nor love,
because they put you
also in a box,
know that your God broke free
and ran away.
So send your spirit

then, to dance with her.
Dance, sing with the God
whom they cannot tame nor chain.
Dance within, though they chain
your very guts
to the great stone walls . . .
Dance, beloved,
Ah, Dance!

Edwina Gateley, *I Hear a Seed Growing* (Anthony Clarke Books 1990)

'Oh, if only it were possible to find understanding,' Joseph exclaimed. 'If only there were a dogma to believe in. Everything is contradictory, everything tangential; there are no certainties anywhere. Everything can be interpreted one way and then again interpreted in the opposite sense. The whole of world history can be explained as development and progress and can also be seen as nothing but decadence and meaninglessness. Isn't there any truth? Is there no real and valid doctrine?'

The Master had never heard him speak so fervently. He walked on in silence for a little, then said: 'There is truth, my boy. But the doctrine you desire, absolute, perfect dogma that alone provides wisdom, does not exist. Nor should you long for a perfect doctrine, my friend. Rather, you should long for the perfection of yourself. The deity is within *you*, not in ideas and books. Truth is lived, not taught. Be prepared for conflicts, Joseph Knecht – I can see they have already begun.'

Hermann Hesse, *The Glass Bead Game* (Penguin 1979)

A person must be in contact with his own reality if the Lord is to be real to him.

W. J. Connolly, 'Notes on the Spiritual Exercises' in
Review for Religious (1981)

The blessing of God, the eternal goodwill of God, the shalom of God, the wildness and the warmth of God, be among us and between us, now and always.

Jim Cotter, *Prayer at Night* (Cairns Publications 1988)

6

What might it mean to follow Christ?

That is sanctity: the wholeness of giving the gift of all your self.

Rowan Williams

Jesus responded to God's personal calling to him more fully and completely than anyone. He is the prime example of personal calling. Does that mean we should model our lives on his?

As a youngster I was repelled by the idea of imitating Christ. It conjured up the prospect of a sort of karaoke life, mouthing someone else's words and aping their mannerisms. There are people who think that that is what Christian life is about, and it is so obviously false that it invites the charge that Christianity makes hypocrites of us.

What might a genuine following of Christ involve? I think it means being as generous with our true selves and as lavish with our inner treasure as he was – each of us discovering what we are about and living it with every fibre of our being. What a rich and enriching life it would be; a different calling for every human being! But it would not make for unfailing popularity. We could find that what we also have in common with Jesus in so doing is that we would be a threat to those who are more concerned with power, or status, or material riches. We would be likely, as he did, to incur the envy of those who are not living what they are for, with all that that brings with it.

Something to do

- Take a little uninterrupted time of quiet. When you have settled yourself, close your eyes and picture an inner room, as it were within you. Allow the features of this room to take shape in your mind's eye: take a few minutes to picture it as vividly as you can ... Be there now quietly in your inner room ...

After a few minutes you hear a knocking on your door. It is Jesus. What do you want to say to him? . . . Be as honest with yourself as you can . . . Do you decide to answer the door? . . .

- If so, invite him in and have a frank and open conversation with him. (You may find it a help to do this on paper. Write down what you want to say to him. Then wait for what his reply seems to be and write that down. Then write your honest reply to that, and so on.)
- If not, be aware of why you do not open the door. Write down your reasons.

This is a widely used method of meditation which helps to make Jesus real for you, and helps you to be real with him. This one is based on the words 'behold, I stand at the door and knock' (Revelation 3.20). To get to know Jesus better, try using this method with passages from the Gospels. Choose an event from a Gospel, picture the scene, and let your imagination re-create the event with you taking part in it, interacting with Jesus and the people with him.

It helps if you have a trusted and godly person whom you could meet with now and then, to whom you can describe what happens and how you feel in these meditations, and who can if necessary give you some guidance.

One should make clear to oneself what it means when God becomes man. It means nothing less than a world-shaking transformation of God. It means more or less what Creation meant in the beginning, namely an objectivation of God. At the time of the Creation he revealed himself in Nature; now he wants to be more specific and become man.

C. G. Jung, *Answer to Job*

[Jesus] was in the form of God; yet he laid no claim to equality with God, but made himself nothing, assuming the form of a slave. Bearing the human likeness, sharing the human lot, he humbled himself, and was obedient, even to the point of death, death on a cross!

Philippians 2.6–8 (REB)

There are those who try to be like Jesus ... There is just enough in the Scriptures to give some support to this position (Eph. 5.1; Phil. 3.17; 1 Pet. 2.21). But there are more passages which seem to express another point of view (e.g. Phil. 2.12–13; Col. 1.27). We see in Jesus Christ the one who is the true man, the genuine man, the man for others, and what it means to be fully human. There are others who have entered into the family likeness of Jesus Christ. We need to know them, to see them, and such people are guides. But we are never to imitate them in the sense of becoming a copy of another person, not even Christ. We are to *abide* in Christ. We are to believe, to receive, and to let him take up his abode in us and bring to fullness our own unique being. It does not involve copying a perfect standard, which, though terribly difficult, is relatively safe.

What is really involved in being a Christian is far more difficult and exciting and frightening. It is to let Jesus Christ actually be within us and resuscitate within us all those wild hopes the world has taught us to distrust. It is the willingness to live without the security of the law, to live daringly without demanding answers, without having to know right and wrong. It is a matter of knowing that no matter what mistakes I make as I seek to maintain my relationship with him, there will always be another chance. It is to let him revive those great expectations that quietly disappeared when I learned to be 'realistic' about my limitations. It is to let the very word of God in Jesus Christ call to life the dead within me. It is to let him call me into being.

Gordon Cosby, *Handbook for Mission Groups* (Word Books 1975)

Their admiration was unbounded. 'He has done all things well,' they said, 'he makes the deaf hear and the dumb speak.'

Mark 7.37

Jesus had now finished what he wanted to say, and his teaching made a deep impression on the people because he taught them with authority, and not like their own scribes.

Matthew 7.28–9

Going from that district, he went to his home town and his disciples accompanied him. With the coming of the sabbath he began teaching in the synagogue and most of them were astonished when they heard him. They said, 'Where did the man get all this? What is this wisdom that has been granted him, and these miracles that are worked through him? This is the carpenter, surely, the son of Mary, the brother of James and Joset and Jude and Simon? His sisters, too, are they not here with us?' And they would not accept him.

Mark 6.1–3

Now on another sabbath he went into the synagogue and began to teach, and a man was there whose right hand was withered. The scribes and the Pharisees were watching him to see if he would cure a man on the sabbath, hoping to find something to use against him. But he knew their thoughts; and he said to the man with the withered hand, 'Stand up! Come out into the middle.' And he came out and stood there. Then Jesus said to them, 'I put it to you: is it against the law on the sabbath to do good, or to do evil; to save life, or to destroy it?' Then he looked round at them all and said to the man, 'Stretch out your hand.' He did so, and his hand was better. But they were furious, and began to discuss the best way of dealing with Jesus.

Luke 6.6–11

That is sanctity: the wholeness of giving the gift of all your self.

Rowan Williams, *Open to Judgement* (DLT 1994)

You compel many to change their opinion about you; they hold that very much against you. You approached them and yet went on past them: that they will never forgive you.

You go above and beyond them: but the higher you climb, the smaller you appear to the eye of envy. And he who flies is hated most of all.

Friedrich Nietzsche, *Thus Spoke Zarathustra*

Now it was the governor's custom at the Feast to release a prisoner chosen by the crowd. At that time they had a notorious prisoner, called Barabbas. So when the crowd had gathered, Pilate asked them, 'Which one do you want me to release to you: Barabbas, or Jesus who is called Christ?' For he knew it was out of envy that they had handed Jesus over to him.

Matthew 27.15–18 (NIV)

God does not explain why there is suffering – God suffers alongside us. God does not explain why there is sorrow – God became the sorrowful one. God does not explain why there is humiliation – God practises self-emptying love. We are no longer alone in our vast loneliness. God is with us. We are no longer in solitude, but rather in solidarity. The arguments from reason are silenced. It is the heart that speaks. It tells of a God who does not ask questions but who acts, who does not offer explanations but lives out an answer.

Leonardo Boff, *The Path to Hope* (Orbis 1993)

The Musician

A memory of Kreisler once:
At some recital in this same city,
The seats all taken, I found myself pushed
On to the stage with a few others,
So near that I could see the toil
Of his face muscles, a pulse like a moth
Fluttering under the fine skin
And the indelible veins of his smooth brow.

I could see, too, the twitching of the fingers,
Caught temporarily in art's neurosis,
As we sat there or warmly applauded
This player who so beautifully suffered
For each of us upon his instrument.

So it must have been on Calvary
In the fiercer light of the thorns' halo:
The men standing by and that one figure,
The hands bleeding, the mind bruised but calm,
Making such music as lives still.
And no one daring to interrupt
Because it was himself that he played
And closer than all of them the God listened.

R. S. Thomas, *Collected Poems 1945–1990* (Dent 1993)

Now on that same day two of them were going to a village called Emmaus, about seven miles from Jerusalem, and talking with each other about all these things that had happened. While they were talking and discussing, Jesus himself came near and went with them, but their eyes were kept from recognizing him. And he said to them, 'What are you discussing with each other while you walk along?' They stood still, looking sad. Then one of them, whose name was Cleopas, answered him, 'Are you the only stranger in Jerusalem who does not know the things that have taken place there in these days?' ... Then he said to them, 'Oh, how foolish you are, and how slow of heart to believe all that the prophets have declared! Was it not necessary that the Messiah should suffer these things and then enter into his glory?'

Luke 24.13–18, 25–6 (NRSV)

Everyone moved by the Spirit is a son of God. The spirit you received is not the spirit of slaves bringing fear into your lives again; it is the spirit of sons, and it makes us cry out, 'Abba, Father!' The Spirit himself and our spirit bear united witness that we are children of God. And if we are children we are heirs as well: heirs of God and coheirs with Christ, sharing his sufferings so as to share his glory.

Romans 8.14–17

[Christianity has recognized] Christ as the one and only God-man. But the indwelling of the Holy Ghost, the third Divine Person, in man, brings about a Christification of many, and the question then arises whether these many are all complete God-men. Such a transformation would lead to insufferable collisions between them, to say nothing of the unavoidable inflation to which the ordinary mortal, who is not freed from original sin, would instantly succumb. In these circumstances it is well to remind ourselves of St. Paul and his split consciousness: on one side he felt he was the apostle directly called and enlightened by God, and, on the other side, a sinful man who could not pluck out the 'thorn in the flesh' and rid himself of the Satanic angel who plagued him. That is to say, even the enlightened person remains what he is, and is never more than his own limited ego before the One who dwells in him, whose form has no knowable boundaries, who encompasses him on all sides, fathomless as the abysms of the earth and vast as the sky.

C. G. Jung, *Answer to Job*

The majority of American Christians have had enough catechism or confirmation classes to know the paradoxical Christian doctrine that Jesus is both human and divine ... They then put 99.5 percent of their money on his divinity and 0.5 percent on his humanity. It is a most comfortable disproportion. It puts Jesus way up there in the clouds, seated at the right hand of the Father, in all his glory, 99.5 percent divine, and it leaves us way down here on earth scratching out a very ordinary existence according to worldly rules, 99.5

percent human. Because that gulf is so great, American Christians are not seriously encouraged to attempt to bridge it. When Jesus said all those things about being the way and that we are to take up our cross and follow him, and that we were to be like him and might even do greater things than he did, he couldn't possibly have been serious, could he? I mean, he was divine, and we're just human. So it is, through the large-scale ignoring of Jesus' very real humanity, that we are allowed to worship him in name without the obligation of following in his footsteps.

M. Scott Peck, *A Different Drum*

The great objection brought against Christianity in our time, and the real source of the distrust which insulates entire blocks of humanity from the influence of the Church, has nothing to do with historical or theological difficulties. It is the suspicion that our religion makes its followers *inhuman*.

'Christianity', so some of the best of the Gentiles are inclined to think, is bad or inferior because it does not lead its followers to levels of attainment beyond ordinary human powers; rather it withdraws them from the ordinary ways of humankind and sets them on other paths. It isolates them instead of merging them with the mass. Instead of harnessing them to the common task, it causes them to lose interest in it. Hence, far from raising them to a higher level, it diminishes them and makes them false to their nature.

Teilhard de Chardin, *Le Milieu Divin* (Collins 1964)

Jesus our brother,
you followed the necessary path
and were broken on our behalf.
May we neither cling to our pain
where it is futile,
nor refuse to embrace the cost
when it is required of us;
that in losing our selves for your sake,
we may be brought to new life.

Janet Morley, *All Desires Known* (SPCK 1992)

7

Seek wholeness

All of us need help at least some of the time.

Arnold and Amy Mindell

Every now and then, as the centuries pass, the notion of human perfectibility emerges as an ideal to admire and to strive for. You can see it in the sculpture of the ancient Greeks, in the way they idealized the human physical form. It emerges again in painting and sculpture at the time of the Renaissance in Europe: for example the Michelangelo David – the human being as Greek god, physically flawless. It is present today in the images dangled in front of our eyes by advertisers, and in the various therapies and nostrums that promise to remove all blemishes, from your skin and from your soul. In Christian circles it appears as the search for total healing of body and mind, where healing means getting rid of all the wounds and imperfections, as though they were somehow removable without trace.

I am all for that where it is possible. But for many people it is not possible. For most of us 'healing' is more like coming to some sort of terms with our wounds and disabilities, rather than simply being able to be rid of them. Wholeness is more often about the integration of all that we are than about getting rid of things. Becoming a perfect specimen of humanity is not the overriding purpose of life. Being generous with what we are is. But you cannot give what you have not yet accepted.

Most of us need help with this at some stage. This is not because we are all emotionally scarred or handicapped in any obvious way (though perhaps more of us are than realize it). It is that the commonly accepted notion of normality – conformism, not rocking the boat, not taking any chances, not speaking out of turn, etc. – stunts our capacity to be the loving and creative people God invites us to be. It is as if inside our adult bodies we are still children at school who have had drummed into us that there is a proper kind of person to be and a proper way to do things, and that if you step out of line there will be trouble. But God's personal calling to you will always involve some kind of risk-taking and stepping out of line.

Something to do

- What aspect of yourself or your nature or your personal history do you find it hardest to accept or feel most limited by?
- Might it be possible to come to better terms with it?
- Is there someone whose wisdom you trust who could help you to find a way of doing this?

◆

Some time after this there was a Jewish festival, and Jesus
went up to Jerusalem. Now at the Sheep Pool in Jerusalem
there is a building, called Bethzatha in Hebrew, consisting of
five porticos; and under these were crowds of sick people
– blind, lame, paralysed – waiting for the water to move; for
at intervals the angel of the Lord came down into the pool,
and the water was disturbed, and the first person to enter the
water after this disturbance was cured of any ailment he suffered from. One man there had an illness which had lasted
thirty-eight years, and when Jesus saw him lying there and
knew he had been in this condition for a long time, he said,
'Do you want to be well again?'

John 5.1–7

The shadows of the night were broad and black. All through
the cold and restless interval, until dawn, they once more
whispered in the ears of Mr Jarvis Lorry – sitting opposite
the buried man who had been dug out, and wondering what
subtle powers were for ever lost to him, and what were cap-
able of restoration – the old inquiry:–
  'I hope you care to be recalled to life?'
  And the old answer:–
  'I can't say.'

Charles Dickens, *A Tale of Two Cities* (Thomas Nelson, no date)

Healing is really a very limited idea. It deals only with cause and effect. It has little art to it. It does not focus on my ability to dance and move, my ability to visualize, or the creativity of the force behind the symptom.

We all fear our symptoms and want to heal them. We go to all kinds of healers, not realizing that our worst problem is not the sickness, but that we are hypnotized by culture into believing that what we experience is bad and has to be repressed and healed instead of lived and loved.

Arnold and Amy Mindell, *Riding the Horse Backwards*

The Western individual ... not only accepts the herd values of his society but he has invented psychoanalysis to prevent him from straying from them ... The stresses that modern life often produce in sensitive and intelligent people are no longer considered to call for a change in society; it is the individual who is wrong and he consequently becomes a neurotic, not a revolutionary. No more remarkable device than psycho-analysis has ever been devised by a society for preventing its superior citizens from giving it pain.

E. Knight, *The Objective Society* (George Braziller 1960)

High on the list of those great nineteenth-century church-men who might rightly be said to deserve the name of 'saint' must surely stand the Abbé Huvelin [who] bore the load of the spiritual direction of countless people . . .

Huvelin ministered in circumstances of chronic and debilit-ating ill-health. But less well known are the facts documented in the most recent French monograph on his life and work. It is not surprising to discover from his private letters and journals that he suffered acutely from depression. More dis-turbing is the knowledge that the thought of suicide was a recurrent obsession (the word is not too strong). And most startling of all is a section of one of his notebooks, eleven pages long; every page is covered with his signature, scrib-bled again and again, in various forms, interspersed with chilling little phrases. '*Il n'est*': he does not exist. The con-jugation of the imperfect tense: '*J'étais, tu étais, il était*': I used to be . . . Huvelin, in other words, was not what many would call a whole man . . .

The question I want to put is this; can we, with our rhetoric of the identity of holiness and wholeness, begin to cope with the 'sanctity' of a man whose mental and emo-tional balance was so limited? . . . We talk very often as though the creative love of God could work through us only if we removed the fear and self-hatred, the pathological guilt, which stifle the freedom of love . . .

Yet here we have a man whose love is very far from stifled – who, whatever his inner condition, actively transformed the lives of those who came into his ambience.

Rowan Williams, *Open to Judgement*

Take yourselves for instance ... at the time when you were called: how many of you were wise in the ordinary sense of the word, how many were influential people, or came from noble families? No, it was to shame the wise that God chose what is foolish by human reckoning, and to shame what is strong that he chose what is weak by human reckoning; those whom the world thinks common and contemptible are the ones that God has chosen.

1 Corinthians 1.26–8

What is it that makes a person whole in their compassion, their alertness? The Christian can only reply that it is Jesus: there are Christians simply because of a transaction of rejecting violence transformed into an unconditional gift. Because of his loss and dereliction, Jesus gives himself in complete poverty of spirit and abandonment to his Father, to be given to the whole creation ... We believe not because our scars are magically wiped away, but because we see and feel love and enrichment poured into our emptiness from the acknowledged, manifest poverty of another ... From Christ's dread and humiliation flows the grace that can work in all dread and humiliation. It does not demand from us passivity, resignation, but the acceptance that will turn us in a new enlightened understanding to the crooked heart of our neighbour; so that my memory of privation and hurt itself becomes part of what I can offer, in intelligent compassion, to the hurts of others. That is sanctity: the wholeness of giving the gift of all your self. Not waiting till that self is fine and moral and healthy and balanced enough to expose. And if there *is* healing or growth towards integration, perhaps it can only come *in* the giving.

Rowan Williams, *Open to Judgement*

To enter the darkness in trust is to emerge more whole ...

To go further into the inner caverns of badness and self-hatred, with steadiness and courage, is to emerge into a broad place ...

a place of greater honesty and clarity in encounters with others ...

a place of greater willingness to meet others who are very different ...

a place of greater ability and enjoyment in loving and being loved by friends ...

a place of greater strength and compassion ...

Jim Cotter, Prayer at Night

Through love thorns become roses, and
Through love vinegar becomes sweet wine,
Through love the stake becomes a throne,
Through love the reverse of fortune seems good fortune,
Through love a prison seems a rose bower ...
Through love ghouls turn into angels ...
Through love sickness is healthy ...

Jalaludin Rumi (tr. E. H. Whinfield 1881)

Grandfather,
Look at our brokenness.

We know that in all creation
Only the human family
Has strayed from the Sacred Way.

We know that we are the ones
who are divided
And we are the ones
Who must come back together
To walk in the Sacred Way.

Grandfather,
Sacred One,
Teach us love, compassion, and honour
That we may heal the earth
And heal each other.

Ojibway people of Canada

8

'Disabilities' might become gifts

I thank God for my handicaps; for through them I have found
myself, my work, and my God.

Helen Keller

As a child I was subjected to toxic doses of dutiful Christianity. In
fact, as I have already indicated, that was my motive for offering
myself for ordination. I had no personal desire to be ordained. The
whole notion repelled me. It was solely a sense of duty that drove
me to it. So it was that during my twenty years or more as a parish
priest I thought long and deeply about vocation and the calling of
God, and wrestled with questions like, What is it to be truly called
by God? What sort of things does he call people to? Are they always
painful and unwelcome? Or – a wild hope! – could it be that the
calling of God might sometimes chime in with a person's deepest
longings?

Do I regret that period of my life? Whatever I felt at the time,
how could I regret it now? It has been the means by which I have
come to a fuller life than I could possibly have dreamed of. And I
do not think that I personally could have come to it any other way.
It was a journey that had to be taken, a journey of discovery that
the gospel is *good* news and not just a heavy load of unwelcome
obligations.

Some may think that life should not be like this, that such a leaden
notion of the calling of God was little short of neurotic. In fact there
may be dark mutterings from some that even such a call itself was
mere neurosis, not the calling of God at all. I might have thought
that at one time; but not any more. I have come to realize that it is
fairly typical of the sort of way we stumble upon our personal calling. So very often it arises at the point of something we think of as
a wound or disability or a handicap or a problem. As we wrestle
with it and perhaps struggle to be free of it we may find that it has

74

something to give us. And as we begin to come to some sort of wry terms with it, we discover that it contains hidden gold, the beginnings of a personal call from God.

To reflect on

- Do you have to cope with anything that you think of as a problem or disability or handicap?
- Have there been occasions when you have recognized that it is in a way a gift?

———— ✦ ————

There was once a rich and powerful king who had a large and very unusual ruby that was beyond price. This jewel was the basis of his renown, wealth and power. Each day he would gaze at it with great pride. One day, to his utter consternation, he saw that the ruby had upon it a scratch. Horror of horrors! What was he to do?

He called each of his palace jewellers to come and examine the scratch and see what could be done to repair it. They were unanimous that nothing could be done without causing further damage.

The king was devastated, and offered a substantial reward to any jeweller who could be found who could repair the king's ruby. Several jewellers came who fancied their chances, but all confessed that there was indeed nothing that could be done.

Some days later one of the king's servants said that he had heard tell of an old retired jeweller in a remote country district who was said to be very experienced in working with damaged gems. So he was duly sent for; and a few days later he arrived, a little bent old man, rather shabbily dressed. The king's courtiers were very scornful and told the king he was wasting his time. But the king insisted that the old man be shown the damaged gem. He looked at it thoughtfully for some time, and then said to the king, 'I cannot repair your ruby, but if you wish, I can make it more beautiful.' The king was a bit sceptical, but he was desperate to have something done; so he agreed. So the old jeweller set to work, cutting and polishing. Some days later he returned. Upon the king's precious stone he had carved the most delicate rose, its stem being formed by the scratch.

The larger sorrows do not so readily go away, and may be intricately related to the work we are to do ...

The relationship between pain and vocation first became clear to me when I was reading books on child development. In one book an author stated matter-of-factly that play is to a child what work is to an adult. In a very different book on play therapy another author explained how, in arranging dolls and toy furniture, the child expresses her inner conflicts and her struggle to work them out. Is it possible that the adult, when working at what he wants to do, is also engaged in the same process? For such an adult his work becomes his play. Through that work not only is he healed, but he becomes a healer. It might be said that in finding vocation one discovers how to be at play in the world.

Elizabeth O'Connor, *Cry Pain, Cry Hope*

Listen to the language of your wounds.

Jim Cotter, *Prayer at Night*

The more we discover the different degrees and different aspects of our own unhappiness the greater our capacity to sympathize instinctively or to reach out to someone in distress.

Brian Keenan, *An Evil Cradling*

Loneliness is the minister's wound not only because he shares in the human condition, but also because of the unique predicament of his profession. It is this wound which he is called to bind with more care and attention than others usually do. For a deep understanding of his own pain makes it possible for him to convert his weakness into strength and to offer his own experience as a source of healing to those who are often lost in the darkness of their own misunderstood sufferings. This is a very hard call, because for a minister who is committed to forming a community of faith, loneliness is a very painful wound which is easily subject to denial and neglect. But once the pain is accepted and understood, a denial is no longer necessary, and ministry can become a healing service.

Henri Nouwen, *The Wounded Healer* (Doubleday 1972)

So stand still with your wounds and your damage and your weapons and all the baggage of your life. Flawed as you are you stand on holy ground. Your life so far is the earth you stand on, upright to heaven. This is the ground that God has cleared for you. Moses stood and faced God on desert ground. He was a fugitive from the murder of his youth, exiled and in danger. There was blood on the ground, blood on his hands. He knew that he had killed and could kill again. Yet there was the place he had to face God. This was the holy ground, the burning ground. The space between earth and heaven . . .

   This is the blessed space, the space that God the creator hollows out for you, the place where his word is spoken and heard, a space which neither darkness nor chaos can finally overwhelm.

   God meets you here, and nowhere else.

Angela Tilby, *Let There Be Light* (DLT 1989)

9

Know yourself loved by God

You are precious in my eyes . . . and honoured, and I love you.

Isaiah

St Paul claimed, on the authority of Jesus, that it is more blessed to give than to receive. The fact is, many of us find it *easier* to give than to receive, perhaps because of our past experiences of receiving love – or of not receiving it. I am reminded of a young woman in an apparently good marriage, who was in hospital having her first baby. Her husband was not able to be there. Instead, out of the blue a note arrived on the day of the birth saying he was leaving her for someone else. It was several years before she felt she could even contemplate trusting a man again. We all long for love, to love and to be loved, but many hurts and traumas stand in the way. And of course our human experience colours also our expectations of God. For many it needs courage to open themselves to the love of God.

To reflect on

- Look back over your life at your experiences of receiving, or not receiving, love, from your childhood onwards (perhaps you have been doing this with the help of a skilled counsellor or a good listener).
- Does what happened to you in your past affect your expectation of the quality of God's love?

———— ◆ ————

We cannot transform our lives, unless we allow them to be transformed by that stroke of grace. It happens; or it does not happen. And certainly it does *not* happen if we try to force it upon ourselves, just as it shall not happen so long as we think, in our self-complacency, that we have no need of it. Grace strikes us when we are in great pain and restlessness. It strikes us when we walk through the dark valley of a meaningless and empty life. It strikes us when we feel that our separation is deeper than usual, because we have violated another life, a life which we loved, or from which we were estranged. It strikes us when our disgust for our own being, our indifference, our weakness, our hostility, and our lack of direction and composure have become intolerable to us. It strikes us when, year after year, the longed-for perfection of life does not appear, when the old compulsions reign within us as they have for decades, when despair destroys all joy and courage. Sometimes at that moment a wave of light breaks into our darkness, and it is as though a voice were saying: 'You are accepted. *You are accepted*, accepted by that which is greater than you, and the name of which you do not know. Do not ask for the name now; perhaps you will find it later. Do not try to do anything now; perhaps later you will do much. Do not seek for anything; do not perform anything; do not intend anything. *Simply accept the fact that you are accepted!*' If that happens to us, we experience grace.

Paul Tillich, *The Shaking of the Foundations* (Penguin 1962)

You are my son [my daughter], my beloved, I delight in you.

Mark 1.11 (tr. ed.)

Accustom yourself to the wonderful thought that God loves you with a tenderness, a generosity, and an intimacy which surpasses all your dreams. Give yourself up with joy to a loving confidence in God and have courage to believe firmly that God's action towards you is a masterpiece of partiality and love . . .

Rejoice that you are what you are; for our Lord loves you very dearly. He loves the whole of you, just as you are.

Abbé de Tourville, *Letters of Direction* (Dacre 1939)

What is emerging and is so marvellous is the feeling of being wholly loved. I suppose when I lost my mother I lost that feeling. I have marvellous other loves – my husband, my father, very special friends – so I'm not short of love by any means. My mother's love was always very important to me and it was removed, so I suppose I was searching for a substitute. Now I'm beginning to realize there is no love in the outside world which can provide you with the sense of being totally loved except the Christ love. There is no other base on which you can walk forward into the dark. But it's a relatively new thing to discover this divine love within, love which sees you at every moment, every second of the day, and which accepts you as you are. I now have so much more confidence in myself as a person and as a performer because I feel totally loved within. And because I am beginning to learn to love myself as I am, I hope very much I am beginning to love my neighbour. I think, for me, it has to work in that direction.

Dame Janet Baker, singer, at the Canterbury Diocesan Conference (Sept. 1984)

Yes, there is that voice, the voice that speaks from above and from within and that whispers softly or declares loudly: 'You are my Beloved, on you my favor rests.' It certainly is not easy to hear that voice in a world filled with voices that shout: 'You are no good, you are ugly; you are worthless; you are despicable, you are nobody – unless you can demonstrate the opposite.'

These negative voices are so loud and so persistent that it is easy to believe them. That's the great trap. It is the trap of self-rejection. Over the years, I have come to realize that the greatest trap in our life is not success, popularity or power, but self-rejection. Success, popularity and power can, indeed, present a great temptation, but their seductive quality often comes from the way they are part of the much larger temptation to self-rejection. When we have come to believe in the voices that call us worthless and unlovable, then success, popularity and power are easily perceived as attractive solutions. The real trap, however, is self-rejection. I am constantly surprised at how quickly I give in to this temptation. As soon as someone accuses me or criticizes me, as soon as I am rejected, left alone or abandoned, I find myself thinking: 'Well, that proves once again that I am a nobody.' Instead of taking a critical look at the circumstances or trying to understand my own and others' limitations, I tend to blame myself – not just for what I did, but for who I am. My dark side says: 'I am no good ... I deserve to be pushed aside, forgotten, rejected and abandoned.'

Maybe you think that you are more tempted by arrogance than by self-rejection. But isn't arrogance, in fact, the other side of self-rejection? Isn't arrogance putting yourself on a pedestal to avoid being seen as you see yourself?

Henri Nouwen, *Life of the Beloved* (Hodder & Stoughton 1992)

And he showed me more, a little thing, the size of a hazelnut, on the palm of my hand, round like a ball. I looked at it thoughtfully and wondered, 'What is this?' And the answer came, 'It is all that is made.' I marvelled that it continued to exist and did not suddenly disintegrate; it was so small. And again my mind supplied the answer, 'It exists, both now and for ever, because God loves it.' In short, everything owes its existence to the love of God.

In this 'little thing' I saw three truths. The first is that God made it; the second is that God loves it; and the third is that God sustains it.

Julian of Norwich, *Revelations of Divine Love* (Penguin 1966)

This love is first experienced as a great awakening. The old mystical authors quoted (or misquoted) the Song of Songs – 'Do not awaken love before its time.' They meant that as there is a time for everything under the sun, so there is a time for the awakening of love. Wait for that time. Don't rush into mystical prayer. Don't think you can awaken it by techniques of breathing or mantra-reciting or anything else. However valuable these may be, they will not of themselves awaken love. Another will awaken love in your heart. At first his call may be frightening; but later you will dance for joy.

William Johnston, *Being in Love* (Collins 1988)

But now, thus says Yahweh,
who created you [Jacob]
who formed you [Israel]

Do not be afraid, for I have redeemed you;
I have called you by your name, you are mine.
Should you pass through the sea, I will be with you;
or through rivers, they will not swallow you up.
Should you walk through fire, you will not be scorched
and the flames will not burn you.
For I am Yahweh, your God,
the Holy One of Israel, your saviour.

I give Egypt for your ransom,
and exchange Cush and Seba for you.
Because you are precious in my eyes,
because you are honoured and I love you,

                                          Isaiah 43.1–4

Love bade me welcome: yet my soul drew back,
                    Guiltie of dust and sinne.
But quick-ey'd Love, observing me grow slack
                    From my first entrance in,
Drew nearer to me, sweetly questioning,
                    If I lack'd any thing.

A guest, I answer'd, worthy to be here:
                    Love said, you shall be he.
I the unkinde, ungratefull? Ah my deare,
                    I cannot look on thee.
Love took my hand, and smiling did reply,
                    Who made the eyes but I?

Truth Lord, but I have marr'd them: let my shame
                    Go where it doth deserve.
And know you not, sayes Love, who bore the blame?
                    My deare, then I will serve.
You must sit down, sayes Love, and taste my meat:
                    So I did sit and eat.

                                George Herbert (1593–1633)

84

From the time these things were first revealed I had often wanted to know what was our Lord's meaning. It was more than fifteen years after that I was answered in my spirit's understanding. 'You would know our Lord's meaning in this thing? Know it well. Love was his meaning. Who showed it you? Love. What did he show you? Love. Why did he show it? For love. Hold on to this and you will know and understand love more and more. But you will not know or learn anything else – ever!'

So it was that I learned that love was our Lord's meaning. And I saw for certain, both here and elsewhere, that before ever he made us, God loved us; and that his love has never slackened, nor ever shall. In this love all his works have been done, and in this love he has made everything serve us; and in this love our life is everlasting. Our beginning was when we were made, but the love in which he made us never had beginning. In it we have our beginning.

Julian of Norwich, *Revelations of Divine Love*

This, then, is what I pray, kneeling before the Father, from whom every family, whether spiritual or natural, takes its name:

Out of his infinite glory, may he give you the power through his Spirit for your hidden self to grow strong, so that Christ may live in your hearts through faith, and then, planted in love and built on love, you will with all the saints have strength to grasp the breadth and the length, the height and the depth; until, knowing the love of Christ, which is beyond all knowledge, you are filled with the utter fullness of God.

Glory be to him whose power, working in us, can do infinitely more than we can ask or imagine; glory be to him from generation to generation in the Church and in Christ Jesus for ever and ever. Amen.

Ephesians 3.14–21

10

God's name for you

Yahweh called me before I was born, from my mother's womb he pronounced my name.

Isaiah

The idea that their name somehow embodies something of a person's essential nature is very ancient. Manifestly, the Christian names or surnames we actually have are not unique. Even if you have several names there is no guarantee that your combination is not also someone else's. It can be quite a shock to find that another person has exactly the same names as you, a sort of affront. It touches and brings to the surface the age-old instinct that you are in fact unique and that your name should encapsulate the essential you-ness of you, which is different from every other human being.

T. S. Eliot plays with this idea of the unique name in *The Naming of Cats*. In Eliot's rhyme, the cat, and only the cat, knows his own 'effanineffable deep and inscrutable singular name'. Ours is perhaps known only to God, for whom our life is one long naming and calling into being. If this is an unfamiliar idea to you, do not dismiss it. As you read the story and the quotations in this chapter, allow the possibility that it might be so.

To reflect on

- Look back over your life so far. Is there something you have done – it might be some quite small thing – which in some way crystallizes for you your sense of who you are?

---◆---

There is an irreducible opposition between the deep tran-
scendent self that awakens only in contemplation, and the
superficial, external self which we commonly identify with
the first person singular. We must remember that this superficial 'I' is not our real self. It is our 'individuality' and our
'empirical self' but it is not truly the hidden and mysterious
person in whom we subsist before the eyes of God. The 'I'
that works in the world, thinks about itself, observes its own
reactions and talks about itself is not the true 'I' that has been
united to God in Christ. It is at best the vesture, the mask, the
disguise of that mysterious and unknown 'self' whom most
of us never discover until we are dead.

Thomas Merton, *Seeds of Contemplation* (Anthony Clarke 1972)

One night Rabbi Yehuda, the greatest rabbi of his age in
Europe, had a dream: he dreamt that he had died and was
brought before the throne of God. The angel who stands
before the throne said to him 'Who are you?' 'I am Rabbi
Yehuda of Prague,' he replied; 'tell me, sir, if my name is written in the book of the names of those who will have a share
in the kingdom.' 'Wait here,' said the angel, 'I am going to
read the names of all those who have died today that are written in the book.' He read the names out, thousands of them,
strange names to the ears of Rabbi Yehuda; and as the angel
read, the rabbi saw the spirits of those whose names had been
called fly into the dazzling light that surrounded the throne.
At last he finished reading, and Rabbi Yehuda's name had not
been called; he wept bitterly and cried out against the angel.
The angel said, 'I have called your name.' 'I did not hear it,'
said the Rabbi. The angel explained, 'In the book are written
the names of all the men and women who have ever lived on
the earth, for every soul is an inheritor of the kingdom. But
many come here who have never heard their true names on
the lips of man or angel. They have lived believing that they
know their names; and so when they are called to their share
in the kingdom, they do not hear their names as their own.
They do not recognize that it is for them that the gates of the
kingdom are opened. So they must wait here until they hear

their names and know them. Perhaps in their lifetime someone has once called them by their right name: here they shall
stay until they have remembered. Perhaps no one has ever
called them by their right name: they shall stay here till they
are silent enough to hear the King of the Universe himself
calling them.'

At this, Rabbi Yehuda woke and, rising from his bed with
tears, he covered his head and lay prostrate on the ground,
and prayed, 'Master of the Universe! Grant me once before I
die to hear my own true name on the lips of my brothers.'

Based on a retelling by Rowan Williams in Open to Judgement

In his essay 'The Cell' (in *Contemplation in a World of
Action*), Merton charts what he believes is the essential
route of the contemplative (and perhaps ultimately of all
human beings), a route downward through loneliness and
acute boredom, to the place where a man or a woman,
deprived of diversion and the constant affirmation of
others, begins to doubt his or her identity. When the 'dis-
ciple', as Merton calls him, reaches the point in which all
illusion is stripped away, and he knows his own weakness,
failure, and despair to the full, then the way is made clear
for the *akmé*, 'the moment of truth', in which a new identity is discovered in God himself.

Monica Furlong, Merton: A Biography (DLT 1985)

You will be called by a new name
that the mouth of the Lord will bestow . . .

Isaiah 62.2 (NIV)

Meister Eckhart said that when he was born all creation stood up and said, 'God is!' I know that for truth, but I cannot imagine writing those words about myself. That I flowed out from God is not deep enough in my unconscious. Most of us have not known that we celebrate God in the world when we celebrate ourselves. If only there were someone to lean over every crib and to whisper into every new pair of ears, 'God is!'

Elizabeth O'Connor, *Cry Pain, Cry Hope*

We also have another name, one which we do not know. You remember the passage in the Book of the Revelation which says that in the Kingdom each will receive a white stone with a name written on it, a name which is known only to God and to him who receives it. This is no nickname, no family name, no Christian name. It is a name, a word, that is exactly identical with us, which coincides with us, which *is* us. We may almost say it is a word which God pronounced when he willed us into existence and which is us, as we are it. This name defines our absolute and unrepeatable uniqueness as far as God is concerned. No one can know the name, as no one can, in the last analysis, know anyone as God knows him; and yet it is out of this name that everything else comes.

Anthony Bloom, *School for Prayer*

Yahweh called me before I was born,
from my mother's womb he pronounced my name.

Isaiah 49.1

I alone know my purpose for you, says the Lord: prosperity and not misfortune, and a long line of children after you.

Jeremiah 29.11 (NEB)

I I

Realize your gifts

Blossom like a rose planted by a stream. Spread your fragrance like incense, and bloom like a lily. Scatter your fragrance; lift your voices in song.

Ecclesiasticus

'I am not gifted like you.' We may not actually say it, but most of us feel it at some time or another. It says nothing about our actual abilities, or lack of them. It usually says more about our lack of affirmation or encouragement. To become aware of our gifts we need acknowledgement of them from others. (We shall come back to this in chapter 17.) When I was a parish priest, we used to have a parish magazine. I remember writing a piece in it about the death of my father in 1976, and getting one or two comments from readers about it. I had been writing parish magazine articles for ten years, but I think that was probably the first time I began to realize, because of what people said, that I might have some kind of gift for writing. We all need feedback from other people in this way. Otherwise we are liable to underrate our gifts – or overrate them, which can be just as unhelpful. Setting about getting this sort of feedback is the first item in Jacqueline McMakin's and Rhoda Nary's checklist which follows below. It is a very perceptive list and well worth spending time on.

There is another route to the identification of gifts, and that is to learn from our envy or admiration of what another person does. This *can* be a clue to our own as yet unlived possibilities. Hence the many stories about long journeys in search of treasure, only to discover that the treasure sought was in some sense 'back at home' all the time.

So much for ways of bringing our latent capabilities to light. But there is more to be said. In the end it is *you* that will be a gift in what you do.

Paul Tournier writes:

I have a friend, a German, who was in a Russian concentration camp at the end of the war. There was in the same camp another prisoner, a young minister who came from the same village and who had been his playmate back in school. Of course they asked many questions of each other. 'What has become of you? Are you married?' asked the pastor. 'Yes,' answered my friend. 'Whoever did you marry, then?' 'Little Elsa . . . you remember her – she was in school with us.' 'Oh! what a beautiful gift God has made you!' It was this last remark which brought my friend to his conversion. Yes, he had been a nominal Christian, like the rest of us, but he had never known God as a personal god. In a moment, by that remark, he saw that his wife was indeed a gift from God.'   *The Meaning of Gifts* (SCM 1964)

A corny story? Maybe, but it points to a very profound truth, the importance of discovering everything as gift. That has really been the underlying theme of the whole of this book up to this point. Paul Tournier again: 'We cannot give that which we have not received.' I like to think of that remark as not so much about transactions as about attitudes. To become generous, giving, fruitful people we need first to learn to receive, to receive *everything* as gift, the world and all that is in it, the people we encounter, our personal history, our inmost nature and character, our wounds and disasters, as well as our joys and capabilities. It is as we learn, not just to accept, but to receive – and as it were to welcome – all that is and all that happens, that we begin to discover how we ourselves might become gifts for others.

Some questions to ponder

- Do you have another person or a small group of people who will listen to you and give you the warmth, acceptance and encouragement necessary for evoking gifts?
- Have you taken the time and solitude necessary to look at and listen to yourself?
- Are you afraid of rejection if you use your gifts or even try them out? Are you allowing only those gifts you think will be accepted to be named and refusing to name the core gifts?
- Does your envy of others focus you on *their* accomplishments rather than allowing you to develop *your* gifts?

- Are you afraid of provoking envy and thus exposing yourself or your gifts to the negative feelings of others?
- Gifts imply specific commitment to use them and accountability for them. Are you avoiding commitment? Why? Do you have a naïve view of creativity as 'fun and games', and do you back off from the pain and work of creativity?
- Are you aware that the new, the innovative, may be threatening to others and put you in tension with them? Are you willing to move through that tension?
- Are you unwilling to exercise a gift until you are mature in it, and expert? If so, is it because you are taking your gifts too seriously? Are you afraid of experimenting, failing, playing, looking silly?
- Are you more concerned with higher wages, another rung on the ladder, and recognition than with a sense of self-worth, growth?

(These questions are from *Doorways to Christian Growth*, Winston Press 1984.)

◆

Honour yourself with humility,
    and give yourself the esteem you deserve.
Who will acquit those who condemn themselves?
    And who will honour those who dishonour
    themselves?

Ecclesiasticus 10.28–9 (NRSV)

A farmer brought home a chick from an eagle's eyrie. Not quite knowing what to do with it, he put it in a chicken run, where it grew up with the chickens. One day a passing traveller saw it, and commented on its presence. 'It's a chicken,' said the farmer: 'Not so,' said the traveller, 'it's an eagle.' And he took it on his wrist and spoke to the great bird. 'You're an eagle,' he said. 'Fly!' But the eagle looked down at the chickens in the run, hopped down and pecked with them. 'You see,' said the farmer, 'I told you so. It's a chicken.'

For the next week the traveller called each day and brought such food as is proper to an eagle, raw meat and flesh. Slowly the bird's strength began to revive.

So again the traveller took the bird on his wrist and spoke to it: 'You're an eagle,' he said. 'Fly!' and the great bird stretched his wings, but when he saw the chickens in the run, he hopped down and scratched with them. 'You're wasting your time,' said the farmer, 'I told you. It's a chicken.'

Next morning while it was still dark the traveller returned, and taking the bird on his wrist he walked a little way into the bush. As the morning sun rose and tipped with a golden light the great crag where the eagles' eyrie was built, he lifted the bird and pointed to the mountain top: 'You're an eagle,' he said. 'Fly!' And the great bird looked up to the top of the crag, stretched his wings and flew, round and round and round . . . until he vanished in the sky.

A fable told to African audiences by James Aggrey in the 1920s

Perhaps I am stronger than I think.

Perhaps I am even afraid of my strength, and turn it against myself, thus making myself weak. Making myself secure. Making myself guilty.

Perhaps I am most afraid of the strength of God in me. Perhaps I would rather be guilty and weak in myself, than strong in Him whom I cannot understand.

Thomas Merton, *Conjectures of a Guilty Bystander* (Sheldon Press 1977)

Our deepest fear is not that we are inadequate.
Our deepest fear is that we are powerful beyond measure.
It is our light, not our darkness, that most frightens us.
We ask ourselves
'Who am I to be brilliant, gorgeous, talented, fabulous?'
Actually, who are you not to be?
You are a child of God.
Your playing small does not serve the world.
There's nothing enlightened about shrinking
so that other people won't feel insecure around you.
We are all meant to shine as children do ...
And as we let our own light shine, we unconsciously
give other people permission to do the same.

Marianne Williamson

A friend said to me the other day that she has difficulty with the idea of being special or different. She quoted Esther de Waal, 'Only after we have given up the desire to be different and admit that we deserve no special attention is there space to encounter God.' The kind of specialness she speaks of is superficial and spurious, the way some teenagers want to be 'different', which affects some temperaments more than others. It is a smoke screen for the fear that we are of no importance. It seeks attention to try and convince ourselves that we are of value. In order to encounter God we do indeed have to foreswear this game-playing, and re-own our inner child of the past who feels unloved and neglected still. In contrast to this, the specialness and difference that I am pointing to is the uniqueness that is everybody's birthright. It is nothing to do with status, or popularity, or fame, or drawing attention to ourselves. It will not usually bring you any of these things (and may well bring upon you the opposite). But if it does, 'beware when all speak well of you', says Jesus (Luke 6.26). As another friend once said, people who take the risk of doing what they are for and are regarded by others as leaders will be deified, or crucified, or both.

Francis Dewar

94

Each day the king sat in state hearing petitions and dispensing justice. Each day a holy man, dressed as a beggar, approached the king and without a word offered him a piece of very ripe fruit. Each day the king accepted the 'present' from the beggar and without a thought handed it to his treasurer who stood behind the throne. Each day the beggar, again without a word, withdrew and vanished into the crowd.

Year after year this same ritual occurred every day the king sat in office. Then one day, some ten years after the holy man first appeared, something different happened. A tame monkey, having escaped from the women's apartments in the inner palace, came bounding into the hall and leaped up on to the arm of the king's throne. The beggar had just presented the king with his usual gift of fruit, but this time instead of passing it on to his treasurer as was his usual custom, the king handed it over to the monkey. When the animal bit into it, a jewel dropped out and fell to the floor.

The king was amazed and quickly turned to his treasurer behind him. 'What has become of all the others?' he asked. But the treasurer had no answer. Over all the years he had simply thrown the unimpressive 'gifts' through a small upper window in the treasure house, not even bothering to unlock the door. So he excused himself and ran quickly to the vault. He opened it and hurried to the area beneath the little window. There, on the floor, lay a mass of rotten fruit in various stages of decay. But amidst this rubbish of many years lay a heap of precious stones.

An oyster saw a loose pearl that had fallen into the crevice of a rock on the sea bed. After great effort she managed to retrieve the pearl and place it just beside her on a leaf. She knew that human beings searched for pearls and thought, 'This pearl will tempt them, so they will take it and let me be.' When a pearl diver appeared, however, his eyes were conditioned to look for oysters and not for pearls resting on leaves. So he took the oyster which did not happen to have a pearl and allowed the real pearl to roll back into the crevice in the rock.

In the olden days, when London Bridge was lined with shops from one end to the other, there lived at Swaffham in Norfolk a poor pedlar called John Chapman. He was very poor and only made a living with great difficulty.

One night he had a dream about Old London Bridge, and in the dream he was told that if he went and stood on the bridge a man would tell him how he could become rich. At first he thought nothing of it; but he dreamt the same the next night, and the next.

After dreaming of it the third time he decided he must do something about it. So he set out on foot on the long journey to London. At last, footsore and weary, he stood on the great bridge and saw all the fine shops and the Thames and the ships sailing by. All day long he wandered up and down on the bridge looking at the people and the shops and the river. But no rich man came by. In fact the people he saw, if anything, seemed downhearted and grumbling. The next day, too, he wandered up and down on the bridge, and again heard nothing of any consequence.

On the third day, one of the shopkeepers asked him why he was loafing around: hadn't he any wares to sell?

'No,' said the pedlar.

'And do you not beg for alms?'

'Not so long as I can keep myself,' came the reply.

'Then what are you here for, what is your business?' asked the shopkeeper.

'Well,' said the pedlar, 'to tell the truth, I dreamt that if I came here I would meet a man who would tell me how I could become rich.'

The shopkeeper laughed. 'You must be a right fool to come all this way just because of a dream. Why, only the other night I dreamt I was in a place called Swaffham, which I believe is in Norfolk. In my dream I was in an orchard behind a pedlar's house, and there was this great oak tree. And a voice said that if I dug under the tree I would find a great treasure. But I am not such a fool as to go all the way to Norfolk just because of a dream.'

The pedlar listened with growing amazement. Without a word, he set off home again. He dug beneath the oak tree and found treasure that meant he was never in poverty again.

Once upon a time some members of an Amerindian tribe lived in a village in a hollow in the hills. Sometimes in the evenings round the fire there would be talk of a magic rock called the singing stone. But although everyone had heard of the wonder and the wisdom of the singing stone, no one had ever seen it.

One day a young member of the tribe decided he would set out to find it. He set off first northwards and travelled many miles and spoke to many people, but no one had seen the singing stone. Then he set off to the south. Again he travelled many miles and saw many wonderful sights; but he never found the singing stone. Next he set off westwards in his search, but with the same result. Finally he travelled east. He often heard talk of it but again no one could tell him where it was to be found. So after several years of travelling and wandering he decided to make his way back to his village. As he approached it over the ridge of the surrounding hills he thought he could hear distant shouting and voices. As he drew nearer, the shouting and singing grew louder, and at length he could hear what they were saying. 'Welcome to the singing stone!'

God's work of art.
That's me?
Then Beauty must lie
In the eye of the
Beholder.

I feel more like
One of those statues
Michelangelo left
Half emerging
From the marble block;
Full of potential,
On the verge of life,
But prisoned still
By circumstance and
Fear.

Yet part of me is free –
And you are still creating,
Bringing to life
The promise that is there.

Sometimes by
Hammer blows
Which jar my being,
Sometimes by
Tender strokes half felt
Which waken me to
Life.

Go on, Lord.
Love me into wholeness.
Set me free
To share with you
In your creative joy;
To laugh with you
At your delight
In me,
Your work of art.

Ann Lewin, 'Revelation', in *Candles and Kingfishers* (Ann Lewin 1993)

At the court of Henry II, so the story goes, was a jester with an aptitude for juggling. Whether it was balls, or rings or cups, he could keep half a dozen in the air while at the same time entertaining the court with his antics. But he was not happy at court. He wanted to serve God, and felt that juggling wasn't really the way to do it. So one day he handed in his notice and set off to a nearby monastery to become a monk.

The abbot received him kindly and took him to meet the novice master who was responsible for all new members of the order during their first few years.

The novice master said to him, 'So you're a juggler, are you? Well, you should be good with your hands. Come along with me, and I'll set you to painting some of the capital letters in a manuscript of the Gospels.' But after a few days it became quite clear that he was completely useless when it came to painting. He was used to making lightning-fast movements with his hands, and he couldn't seem to get the hang of the slow and careful ways the brothers painted the capital letters.

'Hm! You don't seem to be much good at this,' said the novice master, 'let's try you in the kitchens.' But the jester was even worse in the kitchens. He couldn't cook at all, and things got so bad that the brothers insisted that someone else should prepare the meals.

So the novice master set him to tending the vegetable plots, but as he had never been in the country before, he didn't know weeds from vegetables, with predictable results!

'Well,' said the novice master, 'There doesn't seem much you can do in a monastery. How about going and sweeping the church – nothing much can go wrong there!'

But it could. The jester wasn't used to brooms, and he knocked a candle off the altar, and broke it. He was very upset about this latest calamity, and felt that there was nothing he could do for God at all. But as he picked up the bits of the candlestick, he remembered that there was one thing he *could* do. The church was so quiet that he was sure God would like it made a bit more joyful, so he began to juggle the pieces of candlestick for God to enjoy.

At that moment, the novice master came in. He was horrified, 'Juggling in church,' he exclaimed, 'disgraceful! Stop it at once!'

Everyone in the industry knew his work. His style was so advanced it created a place of its own. Plenty of people were in positions to use – and benefit from – that quality. But instead, very often, they took pleasure in rejecting it.

Obituary of Tony Cooper, graphic designer (*Guardian*, 9.10.93)

Thought today of envy – the envy of Herod. It is a dread thought that another should take my place – another be considered greater than I. Kill off quickly the possibility of replacement. Secure my own position. Kill off Russia and China and keep America first. Kill the slumbering giant in every nation – better still, kill the slumbering giant in every person.

As for the exercising of gifts, let everyone be cautious. The exercising of gifts evokes envy – makes enemies of those who, if you stay commonplace, would be your friends. Above all, do not exercise the gift of being yourself – this is the greatest threat of all. Kill off the man who would be himself. Watch out, if you plan to be yourself. Such disturbance of the peace will not be allowed in many hearts.

Envy, the killer, strikes not only the head beneath the star, but the one who follows the star. Envy does not know that everyone has a star above their head. Small wonder that I dread my own envy, but then I also dread yours. I will protect us both and keep secret the fact that I am the possessor of gifts. And if you will be so kind, please do the same for me. Or is there another way?

Elizabeth O'Connor, *Eighth Day of Creation*

Once upon a time an elderly couple lived in a little cottage in a wood. He was a woodcutter and they only managed to scrape a living. So they were very poor. The only possession of any value that the man had was a pocket watch which he had inherited from his grandfather. It was his pride and joy, even though it didn't have a chain. The woman's most treasured possession was her lovely long chestnut hair in which she took great joy.

Christmas was coming and each knew in their heart there was going to be no money to spare for presents. But each loved the other very much and each wanted to give the other a very special present.

So, unbeknown to each other, each made secret plans for a present for the other. The woodcutter decided to sell his watch to be able to get his wife a present she could really appreciate. She, for her part, thought long and hard about how she could raise money to get her husband a present that really expressed her love for him. In the end she decided to sell her hair. And she arranged to go out late on Christmas Eve to have it cut.

The great day came and each had lovingly wrapped a little present for the other. He had bought her a tortoiseshell comb to fasten her lovely long hair. She had bought him a gold chain for his watch.

There are those who give little of the much which they have – and they give it for recognition and their hidden desire makes their gifts unwholesome.

And there are those who have little and give it all.

These are the believers in life and the bounty of life, and their coffer is never empty.

There are those who give with joy, and that joy is their reward.

And there are those who give with pain, and that pain is their baptism.

And there are those who give and know not pain in giving, nor do they seek joy, nor give with mindfulness of virtue;

They give as in yonder valley the myrtle breathes its fragrance into space.

Through the hands of such as these God speaks, and from behind their eyes he smiles upon the earth.

Kahlil Gibran, The Prophet (Heinemann 1923)

12

Know the world's needs, feel the world's pain

We cannot dismiss anyone as of no consequence.

Paul Rowntree Clifford

When I went to be vicar of a parish in Sunderland in 1966 one of the first things we noticed was that women of thirty commonly looked as though they were at least fifty. Of the two nations in this country Sunderland belongs to the second. As it turned out, our fifteen years in that parish were quite an education for us, seeing and feeling the effects the industrial revolution has had over the last half-dozen generations since it took hold of people's lives. Sunderland was at that time a town and a people dependent on heavy industry, mainly mining and shipbuilding, with all that follows from that: the vulnerability to recession – when world trade slackens more ships do not need to be built; the macho culture – you have got to be strong in order to do the work; a particular kind of enslavement of women where they have total responsibility for the welfare and survival of all the members of the household including the husband, whether he is in work or not; the way extended families and communities stick together and help each other, for survival when money is short; attitudes to education, which is regarded as basically organized by 'them' for 'them'; the strength and immovability of the social divisions in the country – there were concrete bollards across the middle of the road that connected the council estate and the private estate in our parish, so that you could not drive directly from one to the other, a kind of symbol of the English apartheid; and finally the importance of football. I will never forget 1973 when Sunderland won the FA Cup. The whole mood of the town was lifted for weeks afterwards, people were smiling and cheerful, the calls to the Samaritans plummeted, the place was transformed for everyone, not just the *aficionados*.

For someone with my background, the years I spent in County Durham changed many of my attitudes and assumptions. Your background may be very different, but I think we all in our different ways need to have our eyes opened and our prejudices challenged.

We saw the importance of having our eyes opened in chapter 4 and began to practise it in some small ways. But opening our eyes to the real circumstances and needs of other people may require much undoing of prejudices and the removal of some very sticky labels. The process of opening our eyes is not in this case qualitatively different from what we were exploring in chapter 4. It is basically the same. But in this instance one of the barriers to doing so is self-interest. For example, if we were really to understand how things are for the poor, it would have implications for the taxation and benefit system in this country. The prejudices of the prosperous are mostly kept in place by self-interest and are pathetically pandered to by the press. There is a great deal of money invested in blindness.

As I have been at some pains to explain, God invites each of us to offer something to the life of the world, some activity which will be for the freeing and enlivening and enriching of particular people. His call often comes at the point of an eye-opening encounter with the reality of how things actually are for particular people. It did for Moses (Exodus, chapters 2 and 3), who is one of the chief biblical examples of personal calling. If we are to be open to the calling of God it requires of us an openness to our fellow human beings, to the influences that have shaped them, to the circumstances in which they are set, to the economic, political and social forces that have borne upon their lives; in short, to their real situation. For many of us that requires much effort, and imagination, and generosity of heart, and perhaps years of re-education.

A dozen ways to get started

- Find out as much as you can about the community where you live, the people, their living conditions, their work, their leisure, their background, their feelings about life, their hopes, their values. Talk to as many different kinds of people as you can and listen to their story.
- Learn about the past and present of, for example, Northern Ireland, the former Yugoslavia, Japan, South Africa, one of the countries of Central America, or the former Soviet Union.

- Learn about and if possible visit a Third World country or family.
- Learn more about the arms trade, what Britain exports, who to, and why.
- Subscribe to an informative magazine.
- Simplify your lifestyle.
- Find out who organizes One World Week in your locality and offer to help.
- Join a political party and be active in your membership.
- Join a pressure group and take part in its activities.
- Organize a fast or a pilgrimage.
- Follow closely the views and activities of one MP, or a cabinet minister, or a local councillor. Pray for, question, challenge, support, talk with, provide information for him or her.
- Celebrate! Organize a local festival, or a fun day, or a street party, or participate in an existing one.

----------- ✦ -----------

Court number two is cavernous and tall, like a church nave. Long curtains filter out the light of the morning sun. Barristers in curled wigs and gowns, ruffs and bands and stiff collars, sweep in like clergy, while at the back, on the pews, wait a large but quiet congregation, alone or in family groups, some with their babies, most in their Sunday best. Their air is of tense expectation, of faint hope, of dejection and anxiety. They stand reverently as the registrar strides in, thin-faced, aquiline and bearded.

The cases for the day are all housing cases brought by Hackney Council against tenants in rent arrears, or squatters. The vast majority of the sixty-odd defendants are unrepresented, and the cases are rattled through at the rate of one every five or ten minutes. The defendants step into the box and stand, nervous and alone, relying on memory, emotion, appeal to human fairness. They face a battalion of lawyers and housing officials armed with ribboned briefs, records and regulations. Most of the defendants are on low incomes, some are not getting rent or rate rebates. There are a number of women whose husbands have deserted them, saddling them with rent arrears. But there are also tenants who consider that they, not the council, have a grievance: people who, in total ignorance of the letter of the law, have tried to seek justice in their own manner. Most of these have withheld their rent as a protest against neglected repairs, or as a way of getting back money they claim the council owes them, for damages, or for cash out of their own pocket spent on essential repairs. There are indeed legal ways of doing this, but these people have just gone ahead and taken their own action, and it has rebounded on them. They bring in exhibits like bagfuls of defective plugs, or jam-jars full of cockroaches, to illustrate their points, but they are immaterial to the suit in hand, and the registrar does not even look at them.

Paul Harrison, Inside the Inner City (Pelican 1983)

When two human beings have to settle something and neither has the power to impose anything on the other, they have to come to an understanding. Then justice is consulted, for justice alone has the power to make two wills coincide. It is the image of that Love which in God unites the Father and Son, and which is the common thought of separate thinkers. But when there is a strong and a weak there is no need to unite their wills. There is only one will, that of the strong. The weak obeys. Everything happens just as it does when a man is handling matter. There are not two wills to be made to coincide. The man wills and the matter submits. The weak are like things.

Simone Weil, Waiting on God (Collins 1959)

The law doth punish man or woman
That steals the goose from off the common,
But lets the greater felon loose
That steals the common from the goose.

Anon (eighteenth century)

Please stop, please!
Silence!
Listen to the beating of your heart.
Listen to the blowing of the wind,
the movement of the Spirit.
Be silent – said the Lord –
and know that I am God.
And listen to the cry of the voiceless.
Listen to the groaning of the hungry.
Listen to the pain of the landless.
Listen to the sigh of the oppressed,
and to the laughter of the children.

Celebrating One World (CAFOD 1989)

That evening a television was placed in the far corner of the
room. Sitting in diagonally opposite corners, we could see
the screen but not each other. The guards were out of sight in
another room. The film was the usual Americans-in-Vietnam
story, full of macho posturing and constant slaughter.
Something struck me as I watched this. I was appalled at the
violence of it and yet the movie was no more violent than
anything I had seen previously, perhaps even less so; yet the
violence in it burned deep into me and sickened me. I could
not watch it, I was horrified and ashamed. After it was over
I sat thinking why I had found myself so repelled by what I
had watched. What had changed in me? Perhaps it was a
combination of the futility of the mindless violence in the
film and the way these men were entranced by it. But these
are the reasons of the mind. Something deeper within me
recoiled, aghast and unbelieving at the horror. I could not
understand this passionate revulsion in me.

Brian Keenan, *An Evil Cradling*

Neither had a job. The flat was bare and echoing. In the lounge, only a carpet, a battered sideboard belonging to Tony, and an old television set that can't be used [because the electricity has been cut off]. To sit on, nothing but a bed-spread laid out in one corner. In the kitchen, a gas cooker – an extravagance, bought on hire purchase repaid at £1.88 a week – and a fridge belonging to Tony, but unusable. A bed in one bedroom, a cot in the other.

But the saddest deprivation was for the child. She faced the danger of burns from candles and paraffin heater. She has not a single toy, and no playmates – Julia cannot get her a place in a nursery and won't let her play out because of traffic through the estate. Chantelle was improvising her own amusements, playing with her mother's yellow comb and mirror, stomping round the room in Tony's shoes, babbling to herself while the couple sat and talked in the falling dusk, camped out like war survivors. I asked them how they viewed the future. 'There's nothing you can do,' Tony replied. 'You can raise your voice, but who is listening?'

Paul Harrison, *Inside the Inner City*

Class segregation in Britain ensures that deprivation is well hidden from the more privileged. The capacity for compassion may still be alive, but it never has to see the suffering that could awaken it. The very existence of inner cities and depressed regions as distinct geographical entities militates against policies to assist them. It is perfectly feasible for a suburban or rural resident, a Tory minister or a higher civil servant, to live and die without ever witnessing, let alone understanding, the realities of life on the lower terraces of the social ziggurat.

Paul Harrison, *Inside the Inner City*

Our watchmen are all blind,
they notice nothing.

Dumb watchdogs all,
unable to bark,
they dream, lie down,
and love to sleep.

Greedy dogs that are never satisfied.
Shepherds who know nothing.
They all go their own way,
each after his own interest.

'Come, let me fetch wine;
we will get drunk on strong drink,
tomorrow will be just as wonderful as today
and even more so!'

The upright perish
and no one cares.
Devout men are taken off
and no one gives it a thought.

Isaiah 56.10 – 57.1

A popular Spanish song says in words of marvellous truth: 'If anyone wants to make himself invisible, there is no surer way than to become poor.'

Simone Weil, *Waiting on God*

The Christian gospel declares that people are of inestimable value because they are the children of God, the concern of his love, created for an eternal destiny; not just people in general, but individual men, women and children, each with a name, each having priceless worth. This was made startlingly plain by Jesus when he told his disciples 'the very hairs of your head are all numbered': an extravagant piece of imagery to drive home what he was saying. When we take his words seriously, we begin to realize how far-reaching their significance is. If they are true, if that is how things really are, if God does care for every single man, woman and child in the teeming millions that inhabit the globe, not to speak of the countless generations of the past and those as yet unborn, we cannot dismiss anyone as of no consequence; nor are we entitled to suppose that some are more important than others or that any should be sacrificed to serve some interest which takes precedence over their own inherent worth. The consequences of accepting this basic presupposition are shattering, calling in question not only the way in which we commonly behave towards many of our fellow human beings, but the international, military, political, economic and social policies which have been and still are considered reasonable by those who are responsible for them.

Paul Rowntree Clifford, *Government by the People?* (SCM 1986)

How cruel people become
when animated not by God's Spirit
but by the spirit of getting ahead in the world!

Oscar Romero, Archbishop of San Salvador, in a sermon (5.12.77)

Let me sing to my friend
the song of his love for his vineyard.

My friend had a vineyard
on a fertile hillside.
He dug the soil, cleared it of stones,
and planted choice vines in it.
In the middle he built a tower,
he dug a press there too.
He expected it to yield grapes,
but sour grapes were all that it gave.

He expected justice, but found bloodshed,
integrity, but only a cry of distress.

Isaiah 5.1–2, 7b (the vineyard stands for the nation)

[In Britain] it is totally impossible legally to be 'self-reliant'
if you are dependent on benefit.

Catherine Whiteway (Audenshaw Papers, June 1994)

There is no hidden poet in me, just a little piece of God that
might grow into poetry.

And a camp needs a poet, one who experiences life there,
even there, as a bard and is able to sing about it.

At night, as I lay in the camp on my plank bed, surrounded
by women and girls gently snoring, dreaming aloud, quietly
sobbing and tossing and turning, women and girls who often
told me during the day, 'We don't want to think, we don't
want to feel, otherwise we are sure to go out of our minds,' I
was sometimes filled with an infinite tenderness, and lay
awake for hours letting all the many, too many impressions
of a much too long day wash over me, and I prayed, 'Let me
be the thinking heart of these barracks.' And that is what I
want to be again. The thinking heart of a whole concentration
camp. I lie here so patiently and now so calmly again, that I
feel quite a bit better already. I feel my strength returning to
me; I have stopped making plans and worrying about risks.
Happen what may, it is bound to be for the good.

Etty: A Diary 1941–43

When the lawyer in the Gospel story wanted to invent a pseudo-problem to justify his rather elementary question to Jesus, he asked, 'Who is my neighbour?' The tendency of us Christians, like the lawyer himself, is to limit the answer as far as possible. My neighbour is Christ or my fellow-Christian or – if we have to go beyond the Church – my fellow human beings, or at any rate the more innocent and deserving of them. It simply does not accord with our traditional mentality to define 'neighbour' as 'fellow creature', or to think of the world as including 'world' in its common or garden sense of 'the whole earth'.

John Austin Baker, *Crucible* (April to June 1995)

The environmental crisis that we have reached is of such dimensions that even science is acknowledging that it cannot solve the problems alone ... Five of the most serious aspects of the environmental crisis are population growth, global warming, pollution, the loss of biodiversity and the loss of soil.

Ghillean Prance, Director of Kew Gardens, *Crucible* (April to June 1995)

I recall a young priest from Mississippi who visited the monastery of Gethsemani at the same time I did in the early sixties. This priest spoke with Merton and me about his torment over the segregation of churches in his area. 'I know it's wrong,' he said. 'Sometimes I can hardly face myself in the mirror in the mornings for going along with it. What can I do?'

'Don't do a damned thing,' Merton replied sympathetically. 'Just take the time to become what you profess to be. Then you will know what to do.'

J. H. Griffin, *Thomas Merton: The Hermitage Years*

May the God who dances in creation,
who embraces us with human love,
who shakes our lives like thunder,
bless us and drive us out with power
to fill the world with her justice,
Amen.

Janet Morley, *All Desires Known*

13

Dream dreams

I understand the Christian life to be about the integration of
desire: our personal desires, our political vision, and our longing
for God. So far from being separate or in competition with one
another, I believe our deepest desires spring from the same source.

Janet Morley

What would you do if you won five million pounds on the lottery?
There would be no need for you to go on working to earn your
living. How would you spend your time and energy?

For some of us that is a more difficult question than it sounds.
People whose lives are too full, as they are for many who are in
work at present, usually need uncluttered time and a chance to
reflect before they know what they want to do. While people who
have been made redundant and have all the time in the world may
find they have to wrestle with depression and low self-esteem, as
well as the idiotic rules about being available for non-existent work,
which limits their horizons and their capacity to dream. Others feel
they must have the framework and discipline of going to work;
they feel disorientated and rudderless without it. So for all sorts
of reasons many of us do not find it easy to see visions and conjure
up possibilities. After all, our education system is not too well
geared to helping people to develop their imagination, to encourage
them to think new thoughts and to envisage unexplored ways.

The capacity to imagine and to long for what might be is nevertheless present in all of us, however diffident we may feel about it;
it is one of the distinctive qualities of the human being. There is
within everyone a longing for a new land. It may get trivialized into
wishing for some change of circumstances, or wanting some new
bauble, a car, a kitchen, or a computer. But it seems that, whatever
our circumstances, part of being human is to have this longing
which always draws our hearts to what we hope will be a better

future. For many it never gets beyond a personal hope for themselves and their family. For more generous souls it becomes a hope for others, for humanity, for the world. In the end we find it is the longing for God and his Kingdom.

It is to this hope, that, for example, the Exodus saga speaks, that journey of the Israelites from slavery in Egypt to the Promised Land which is described in the book of Exodus. It is important to see beyond its literal meaning. It is not just about the Jews or the Church. It has a universal significance. It speaks of a journey to be taken by individuals, by nations, by the human race. It is about the promise of God's Kingdom for all, where all can flourish. It is about the journey to a new land where oppression, injustice, selfishness and blindness are no more, a state of both social wholeness and individual fulfilment. It is both a corporate hope for God's world and an exemplar of an individual journey. We are each personally called to set out for a new land. We are each called to unearth our treasure, to live our giftedness, to have a whale of a time doing what we are for and thereby to contribute to the corporate exodus of humanity.

Something to reflect on

- What dreams do you have? If they are for yourself, do they connect with your deepest desires, or are they just daydreams, merely an escape from life's dreariness and frustrations?
- Sooner or later, if we are willing to listen to our deepest longings, they take us beyond ourselves. Give yourself uncluttered time to dream deeply and widely; let your longing feed your imagination. What would you love to see happen? And who would it be for? Who would flourish because of it?

———— ✦ ————

The ... danger of not treating the creative imagination with real love is that this involves a rejection of God – or at least of a huge and magnificent dimension of God. Such a rejection seriously impedes the work of religion in the transformation of the world. Any movement for social change requires a revolution of the imagination ...

Sara Maitland, *A Big-enough God* (Mowbray 1995)

Yahweh said, 'I have seen the miserable state of my people in Egypt. I have heard their appeal to be free of their slave-drivers. Yes, I am well aware of their sufferings. I mean to deliver them out of the hands of the Egyptians and bring them up out of that land to a land rich and broad, a land where milk and honey flow.'

Exodus 3.7–8

The poor and needy ask for water, and there is none,
their tongue is parched with thirst.
I, Yahweh, will answer them,
I, the God of Israel, will not abandon them.

I will make rivers well up on barren heights,
and fountains in the midst of valleys;
turn the wilderness into a lake,
and dry ground into waterspring.

In the wilderness I will put cedar trees,
acacias, myrtles, olives.
In the desert I will plant juniper,
plane tree and cypress side by side.

Isaiah 41.17–19

Then I saw a new heaven and a new earth; the first heaven and the first earth had disappeared now, and there was no longer any sea. I saw the holy city, and the new Jerusalem, coming down from God out of heaven, as beautiful as a bride all dressed for her husband. Then I heard a loud voice call from the throne, 'You see this city? Here God lives among mortals. He will make his home among them; they shall be his people, and he will be their God; his name is God-with-them. He will wipe away all tears from their eyes; there will be no more death, and no more mourning or sadness. The world of the past has gone.'

Then the One sitting on the throne spoke: 'Now I am making the whole of creation new,' he said.

Revelation 21.1–5

Thy Kingdom come! on bended knee
   The passing ages pray;
And faithful souls have yearned to see
   On earth that Kingdom's day:

But the slow watches of the night
   Not less to God belong;
And for the everlasting right
   The silent stars are strong.

And lo, already on the hills
   The flags of dawn appear;
Gird up your loins, ye prophet souls,
   Proclaim the day is near:

The day in whose clear-shining light
   All wrong shall stand revealed,
When justice shall be throned in might,
   And every hurt be healed;

When knowledge, hand in hand with peace,
   Shall walk the earth abroad:
The day of perfect righteousness,
   The promised day of God.

F. L. Hosmer (1840–1929)

The spirit of the Lord Yahweh has been given to me,
for Yahweh has anointed me.
He has sent me to bring good news to the poor,
to bind up hearts that are broken;

to proclaim liberty to captives,
freedom to those in prison;
to proclaim a year of favour from Yahweh,
a day of vengeance for our God,

to comfort all those who mourn and to give them
for ashes a garland;
for mourning robe the oil of gladness,

for despondency, praise.
They are to be called 'terebinths of integrity',
planted by Yahweh to glorify him.

They will rebuild the ancient ruins,
they will raise what has long lain waste,
they will restore the ruined cities,
all that has lain waste for ages past.

Isaiah 61.1–4

My plea ... would be that you should have confidence in yourselves, that you should think (I say think and not just fantasize) deep and big, that for God no 'word,' i.e. action, is impossible, that the urge you feel within yourselves has historical significance, that there where the Spirit is, there is freedom, that real love dispels fear, that once you step out of mediocrity you are saved, that the possibilities are enormous and the world is thirsty for such steps, that you should not just imitate, although you should listen and study, that many 'outsiders' are waiting for such first and courageous steps ... Courage means to put one's own heart into the praxis. I would insist that you are in a privileged position, you are the links with the past and, at the same time, the seeds of the future. But the seeds have to fly with the wind, i.e. to go with the Spirit, in order to fall on other, unknown grounds, and yield fruit.

Raimundo Panikkar, 'Letter to a Young Monk', Living Prayer
(Nov. to Dec. 1986)

A woman dreamt that a new shop had opened in the High Street. Out of curiosity she went in, and to her surprise God was behind the counter. 'Oh,' she said, 'What do you sell here?' 'Everything your heart desires,' said God.

Hardly daring to believe her ears, she decided to ask for everything a person could wish for. 'I want health, and happiness, and wisdom, and peace of mind,' she said. And as an afterthought she added: 'Not just for me and my family, but for everyone in the whole world.' God smiled: 'I think you've got me wrong, my dear,' he said. 'We don't sell fruits here, only seeds.'

The dream of the mighty for more power, of the rich for more wealth, is the nightmare of the powerless and poor. But the dream of the oppressed and poor for liberation is the nightmare of the powerful and rich. It has always been so in a world which is unwilling to share resources and to discern them as gifts not possessions. The dream of the oppressed is utopian, it is a vision of a better world. It is this vision which enabled the first Christians to face persecution. 'Then I saw a new heaven and a new earth.' It is the same vision which has motivated the prophets throughout the centuries, the vision of the kingdom of God inaugurated in Jesus Christ but yet to come in its fullness. This vision threatens those who possess everything except the ability to share with others. The powerful and privileged fear the dreams of the poor and the visions of the prophets because they derive from the coming kingdom of God, God's purpose for his world. They are dreams and visions which are just and right, and will come true.

A nation needs a common vision, a shared dream. A dream which is no-one's nightmare because it promises hope and life in a new way for all. The message of Pentecost is that all people, young and old, Jew and Gentile, black and white, rich and poor, are brought within the scope of God's action through the Spirit. All people may be transformed and so transcend the barriers of race and class which divide nations and turn the dreams of some into the nightmares of others. This is the promise of the gospel in our land, a vision of righteousness and justice. Without such a shared vision the people will perish, and all our dreams will become a nightmare.

John de Gruchy, *Cry Justice* (Collins 1986)

They tell me that one reason for our feeling of economic malaise, in spite of all the statistics telling us that we haven't had it so good for ages, is what they call 'defensive thinking'.

In uncertain times we all try to batten down the hatches, do what we feel safe in doing, and decide to postpone our dreams until the world settles down once more. That's sad, because the world won't go back to where it was, nor will it wait for us to pluck up our courage. And, right now, we need all the dreams we can get. I used to be great at defensive thinking myself. I joined a great international company when I left college and that, I thought, would see me through life. But then I got married. After a couple of years of corporate wifehood, she confronted me one evening – 'Are you happy with your work?' she said. 'It's not the greatest thing in the world,' I said, 'but it's all right'. 'Well, are you proud of it?' 'Not particularly,' I said, 'but I'm not ashamed of it, it's all right.' 'And do you like your colleagues?' 'Oh, they're all right I suppose, harmless anyway.' She looked at me – 'I don't think I want to spend the rest of my life,' she said, 'with someone who is satisfied with "all right". Don't you have any dreams?' 'Well, yes,' I said, 'I've always wanted to be a teacher and a writer.' 'SO', she said, 'when do you resign from *this* job?' Frightening stuff for a defensive thinker, but she was right, absolutely right. If I had stayed, I might now have a nice pension and a golf handicap, but I would be, at heart, a disappointed man.

We can't afford to postpone our dreams, no matter how frightening it might be to take them seriously. In the Gospel of Thomas, yes the Gospel of *Thomas* – that's one of the so-called Gnostic Gospels which were banned, and then hidden, in the days of the early Christian Church – Jesus is recorded as saying, 'If you bring forth what is within you, what you bring forth will save you. If you do *not* bring forth what is within you, then what you do not bring forth will destroy you.' . . .

Reading what is left of their writings, I have a lot of sympathy with some of their insights. Particularly this one – to deny the truth that is in you, is ultimately wrong – for each of us, *and* for the economy.

Charles Handy, in a radio talk

I understand the Christian life to be about the integration of desire: our personal desires, our political vision, and our longing for God. So far from being separate or in competition with one another, I believe that our deepest desires ultimately spring from the same source.

Janet Morley, *All Desires Known*

To see visions or to hear call without being faithful to one's most ardent yearnings is utterly impossible. Our strongest feelings revolve around our wants and desires, and we have been taught since our first summer to give these only slight attention, so that when we think about drawing close to our real longings we have feelings of guilt and shame. It is as though our deepest wishes were unworthy and, if pursued, would get us into all kinds of trouble, and at the very least cause us to feel or be called selfish. The opposite, of course, is true.

Elizabeth O'Connor, *Cry Pain, Cry Hope*

I will stand on my watchtower,
and take up my post on my battlements,
watching to see what he will say to me,
what answer he will make to my complaints.

Then Yahweh answered and said,
'Write the vision down,
inscribe it on tablets
to be easily read,
since this vision is for its own time only:
eager for its own fulfilment, it does not deceive;
if it comes slowly, wait,
for come it will, without fail.'

Habakkuk 2.1–3

People like you must *look* at everything and *think* about it
and communicate with the heaven that dwells deep within
them and listen inwardly for a word to come.

C. G. Jung

Now I am revealing new things to you,
things hidden and unknown to you,
created just now, this very moment,
of these things you have heard nothing until now,
so that you cannot say, 'Oh yes, I knew all this.'

You had never heard,
you did not know,
I had not opened your ear beforehand . . .

Isaiah 48.6b–8a

Listen . . .
to the fragile feelings, not to the clashing fury . . .
to the quiet sounds, not to the loud clamour . . .
to the steady heartbeat, not to the noisy confusion . . .
to the hidden voices, not to the obvious chatter . . .
to the deep harmonies, not to the surface discord . . .

Jim Cotter, *Prayer at Night*

[Abraham's] guest said, 'I shall visit you again next year without fail, and your wife will then have a son.' Sarah was listening at the entrance of the tent behind him. Now Abraham and Sarah were old, well on in years, and Sarah had ceased to have her monthly periods. So Sarah laughed to herself, thinking, 'Now that I am past the age of child-bearing, and my husband is an old man, is pleasure to come my way again!' But Yahweh asked Abraham, 'Why did Sarah laugh and say, "Am I really going to have a child now that I am old?" Is anything too wonderful for Yahweh? At the same time next year I shall visit you again and Sarah will have a son.' 'I did not laugh,' Sarah said, lying because she was afraid. But he replied, 'Oh yes, you did laugh.'

Genesis 18.10–15

Sarah and her husband had had plenty of hard knocks in their time, and there were plenty more of them still to come, but at that moment when the angel told them they'd better start dipping into their old age pensions for cash to build a nursery, the reason they laughed was that it suddenly dawned on them that the wildest dreams they'd ever had hadn't been half wild enough.

Frederick Buechner, *Peculiar Treasures* (Harper & Row 1979)

Thus says Yahweh,
No need to recall the past,
no need to think about what was done before.
See, I am doing a new deed,
even now it comes to light; can you not see it?

Isaiah 43.18–19a

O God,
who set before us the great hope
that your Kingdom shall come on earth
and taught us to pray for its coming:
give us grace to discern the signs of its dawning
and to work for the perfect day
when the whole world shall reflect your glory;
through Jesus Christ our Lord.

Percy Dearmer (1867–1936)

The things, good Lord, that we pray for,
give us the grace to labour for.

Thomas More (1478–1535)

14

Hear a call

You have a duty to perform. Do anything else, do any number of things, occupy your time fully, and yet, if you do not do this task, all your time will have been wasted.
                                                    Jalaludin Rumi

A good example of personal calling is St Paul. The word he uses for it is the Greek word *kharis*. He writes (Ephesians 3.8): 'Although I am the least of all God's people, this grace [*kharis*] was given to me: to preach to the gentiles the unsearchable riches of Christ.' This is not the usual Greek word for call or calling. He is not talking here about the general calling to be a Christian (for which the Greek words he uses are *kaleo and klesis*). Nor is he talking about calling in the institutional sense (i.e. being selected for some official and recognized job, like priest or apostle). In fact he has to go to great lengths to convince the 'proper' apostles that his rather off-beat calling is genuine. Personal calling, both for St Paul and for the rest of us, is in a different realm, a different order of things, as I hope by this time I am managing to convey. The fact that the word *kharis* is used by St Paul to denote his personal calling is worth looking at, since *kharis* is an unusually rich word in Greek and it contains within its various meanings much of what I mean by the phrase 'the personal calling of God'.

First, it means attractiveness, grace of form or speech. When you see someone doing what they are born for, there is always something attractive about it, something winsome and compelling, a sort of innate joyousness or grace, like the exuberant leaping of a springbok. It is obvious that they are doing what they are for.

Second, it means favourable regard towards a person, or, specifically, a favour. God's personal call to you feels like an incredible privilege, a totally unearned gift: 'How is it God can be so good to me?'

Third, it comes to mean the feeling produced by such a favour, i.e. gratitude.

What is not included in the meaning of the Greek word is the fact that God's personal calling to you involves stepping out in a new direction; there is always something fresh and unique about it, and it always involves a risk of some kind. All that is of course manifestly true of St Paul's call to preach the gospel to the gentiles. So St Paul's choice of the word *kharis* for this is richly true to life and to the nature of the personal calling of God for all of us. When we are doing what we are for it is always apparent to those with eyes to see. There is fluency and energy and naturalness in what we do, and light and love shine out from us. That is how it looks from the outside. However much it may cost us (and that is not usually apparent from the outside), the subjective feeling is also that there is a flow about it. It is quite mysterious really, why for *that* person *that* activity has that feel about it. But that is the nature of the personal calling of God. And with it comes a deep sense of joy and fulfilment, leading to a sense of gratitude, a feeling that it is a totally unearned privilege.

There are two particular difficulties in the way of describing what personal calling means. One is that it is infinitely varied; each person's is different. Even if two people are called to what looks outwardly like the same task, the richness that each brings to the doing of it will be different. The second is that the personal calling of God grows and develops in us as we begin to respond. It may begin as the doing of a small kindness, or whispering a word of encouragement, or becoming aware of an inner sense of exuberance and joy and passion in the doing of some task. It could end as a life devoted – in the fullest life-affirming sense of the word – to some particular activity, or some particular group of people. In this book I have tended to pitch it somewhere in the middle of that spectrum and have implied that God's personal calling is to a particular task, perhaps one that you only have time for now and then. That is fine, as far as it goes, and if we respond faithfully it is likely to involve more of our time and commitment as the years go by. But when a person's response becomes ever more whole-hearted, there comes a point where you cannot say that their personal calling is to this or that activity. Their whole life becomes a response to God's personal calling. So it was with Etty Hillesum. You could try and restrict it and say that writing was hers. And, yes, it was, perhaps more than she ever realized, because she died in Auschwitz at the tender age of twenty-eight and all she wrote was her diary and some letters. And what a diary it is – a spiritual classic.

But to limit her personal calling to writing would be a travesty of the truth. In the end her whole life, her being with her fellow Jews in Westerbork camp (to which she went voluntarily), her attitude to life, her every thought, her every breath even, was a response to the personal calling of God. She is not only a prime example of personal calling. Her life illustrates very well the fact that God's personal calling to you simply cannot be reduced to any kind of label. In the end we are talking about the very essence of yourself that needs to become manifest, both in what you are and in the specific things you do. It is nothing to do with 'success', or achievement of any kind: what God will do with your offering is in his hands. It is everything to do with love, loving what you do: and everything to do with what you are and what you do being the generous over-flowing of your deepest nature. The qualities and characteristics of such action (especially by reference to what it is not) are well described by St Paul in the first seven verses of chapter 13 of his first letter to the Corinthians.

Something to do

- Read Luke 4.16–30. In today's world, in your locality, in your experience, who are the impoverished ... the imprisoned ... the blind ... the oppressed? As you reflect on this, who are the particular people whose condition touches your heart most?

  What might they be praying for from God?
  What would it mean for *you* to hear their prayer?

- How do you feel about a personal calling from God to you? As you think about it, which of the following words or phrases apply to you:

  frightened; excited; doubtful; confused; I don't know what to do about it; I don't want to think about it; I am not up to it; I'd like to feel called, but I don't; etc.

- If you do not have any clue about God's calling to you:

  Is something preventing you hearing it?
  Are you taking enough trouble to open your heart and mind to the possibility?
  Are you avoiding something, or running away from something?

- If you do have the beginnings of a sense of calling, write it down as clearly as you can; what do you feel God is nudging you towards? Who would it be for? Where?

I have caught a vision of Christ's new earth and have come to understand that it is every person's vocation to create that earth. We are to cast out demons, be healers, artists, musicians, the builders of caring institutions. Creativity is not the work of a few. We each carry within us the image of God the Creator; we each have the task of making the earth into a fairer, kinder place. The first step is imaging a better world, and that is most apt to happen when we suffer or look on suffering. The difficulty is that we do not take the next step of creating the world we envision. We lack the courage or somehow feel that this is someone else's responsibility rather than the work of the one who sees and images something different and higher.

We are not powerless in the oppressive situations in which we feel caught. We are not bound to the reality we see. We are creators. We can make the new.

Elizabeth O'Connor, Cry Pain, Cry Hope

Vocation . . . has the element of knowing that if you respond to the call, you are faithful to your own inner being and you are enhanced by it. Your own awareness converges with some need out yonder and intersects with it in such a way that you have the sense that you were born to this.

Gordon Cosby, Handbook for Mission Groups

The misery here is quite terrible and yet, late at night when the day has slunk away into the depths behind me, I often walk with a spring in my step along the barbed wire and then time and again it soars straight from my heart – I can't help it, that's just the way it is, like some elementary force – the feeling that life is glorious and magnificent, and that one day we shall be building a whole new world. Against every new outrage and every fresh horror we shall put up one more piece of love and goodness, drawing strength from within ourselves.

Etty: A Diary 1941–43

In the discernment of your call it is not only a matter of 'What do I long to do?' It *can* be worth asking 'What am I running away from? What am I resisting?'

Judith Roark and Myra Flood in conversation

Yahweh said ... 'And now the cry of the sons of Israel has come to me, and I have witnessed the way in which the Egyptians oppress them, so come, I send you to Pharaoh to bring the sons of Israel, my people, out of Egypt.'

Moses said to God, 'Who am I to go to Pharaoh and bring the sons of Israel out of Egypt?' 'I shall be with you,' was the answer.

Exodus 3.9–11

Just now the Lord seems to be calling me to do something about unemployment in the city. First, I'm going to talk about it with many people. I am not just going to say 'Let's discuss it', but 'I am going to do something about it'. I have no idea what I can do or how I can do it, but I see it as a major issue facing our city. If people wonder 'Who do you think you are?', I am just a human being concerned about the dehumanizing effect of unemployment. Many times I've felt a call in that way, right from the founding of the Church of the Saviour to starting the Jubilee Housing Project. What's important is to get started. You may fail; but it's a worse failure to sit back and do nothing. You discover the validation of God's call in actually coming up against objective reality. If there's no response, it may not be my call. Or the call may get modified. In any case, it will get refined as I grapple with it in practice ... Some people hang back from getting into action – 'If only I could find someone else to be with me in this.' Rather, it is a matter of 'I can do all things through Christ who strengthens me.'

Gordon Cosby, (the gist of some remarks in a conversation in 1978)

[One evening] I was part of the volunteer staff of an overnight shelter for street women. It was a very cold night and the women began to arrive early in the evening. The rooms reserved for them were behind the sanctuary of the church and were used for other purposes during the day. Foam rubber mats were laid out over the entire area in one room. Many of the women chose a mat as soon as they arrived. Some had very little with them, though most of them had the bags that have given them the name of bag ladies. One carried her possessions in a child's wagon, and another, more affluent, had hers piled dangerously high in a supermarket cart. The conversation was disconnected, but the atmosphere was warm and peaceful. Each one was given a bowl of stew, bread, and tea . . .

When morning came the peaceful atmosphere inside the shelter turned hostile. Distraught women – some of them old and sick – could not comprehend why they were once more being 'pushed out' into the streets. We who had received them so warmly the night before were the very ones hurrying them along, benefactors so soon become enemies.

In the narrow hall where the women were having breakfast, an old woman with a gentle face kneeled to pray. She was in the way of another woman who taunted her, 'Get up woman. God don't hear your prayer.' The praying woman did not respond and her taunter said again, 'God don't hear your prayer, woman. God don't hear your prayer.'

I asked myself, 'Does God hear her prayer?' Then I remembered. God is in me and where I am God is. The real question was, 'Did I hear her prayer?' What would it mean to hear her prayer?

Elizabeth O'Connor, *Cry Pain, Cry Hope*

Yahweh said to Abram, 'Leave your country, your family and your father's house, for the land I will show you.'

Genesis 12.1

Call more often than not is bound up with economic risks, and often does not seem very prudent to those looking on. A journey is also involved. Call asks that we set out from a place that is familiar and relatively secure for a destination that can be only dimly perceived, and that we cannot be at all certain of reaching, so many are the obstacles that will loom along the way. One of the ways to test the authenticity of call is to determine whether it requires a journey. This journey is not necessarily geographical although, as in the case of Abraham and Moses, it is not at all unusual for it to involve leaving one's work and home. Whether or not the call includes an outward journey, it always requires an inward one. We need to be delivered from all that binds and keeps the real self from breaking into music and becoming joy to the world.

Elizabeth O'Connor, *Cry Pain, Cry Hope*

The world is so much larger than I thought. I thought we went along paths – but it seems there are no paths. The going itself is the path.

C. S. Lewis, *Perelandra* (John Lane 1943)

I have no nostalgia left, I feel at home. I have learned so much about it here. We *are* 'at home'. Under the sky. In every place on earth, if only we carry everything within us.

I have often felt, and I still feel, like a ship with a precious cargo; the moorings have been slipped and now the ship is free to take its load to any place on earth. We must be our own country.

Etty: A Diary 1941–43

Although I am less than the least of all God's people, this grace was given to me: to preach to the Gentiles the unsearchable riches in Christ.

Ephesians 3.8 (NIV)

The person who has found the work that is his or hers to do is at play in the world. Play and vocation are one.

Gordon Cosby, in the Preface to Elizabeth O'Connor, *Cry Pain, Cry Hope*

In the past, ambition stopped me from committing such trivia to paper. Everything had to be marvellous, perfect, I simply could not allow myself to write down any old thing, even though I was sometimes bursting with the longing to do just that.

Etty: A Diary 1941–43

My food is to do the will of the one who sent me, and to complete his work.

John 4.34

Can you and I, who are simple, ordinary people, live creatively in this world without the drive of ambition which shows itself in various ways as the desire for power, position? You will find the right answer when you love what you are doing. If you are an engineer merely because you must earn a livelihood, or because your father or society expects it of you, that is another form of compulsion; and compulsion in any form creates a contradiction, conflict. Whereas, if you really love to be an engineer, or a scientist, or if you can plant a tree, or paint a picture, or write a poem, not to gain recognition but just because you love to do it, then you will find that you never compete with another. I think this is the real key: to love what you do.

To find out what you love to do demands a great deal of intelligence; because, if you are afraid of not being able to earn a livelihood, or of not fitting into this rotten society, then you will never find out. But, if you are not frightened, if you refuse to be pushed into the groove of tradition by your parents, by your teachers, by the superficial demands of society, then there is a possibility of discovering what it is you really love to do. So, to discover, there must be no fear of not surviving.

But most of us are afraid of not surviving, we say, 'What will happen to me if I don't do as my parents say, if I don't fit into this society?' Being frightened, we do as we are told, and in that there is no love, there is only contradiction; and this inner contradiction is one of the factors that bring about destructive ambition.

Krishnamurti, *Think on These Things* (Harper & Row)

Vocation has to do with saving your soul – not by acquiring a secure position of holiness, but by learning to shed the unreality which simply suffocates the very life of the soul . . . Vocation is, you could say, what's left when all the games have stopped.

Rowan Williams, *Open to Judgement*

If we are to make ultimate sense of our lives, all the disparate elements in us have to be integrated around call. The whole life of Jesus revolved around call, as did the life of Moses before him. The theme was in their lives as it is in the life of each of us. We have to deal with it or we become narrow and restrictive, the inevitable price of turning one's back on call – an option that is always present.

Elizabeth O'Connor, *Cry Pain, Cry Hope*

The word of Yahweh was addressed to Jonah son of Amittai: 'Up!' he said, 'Go to Nineveh, the great city, and inform them that their wickedness has become known to me.' Jonah decided to run away from Yahweh, and to go to Tarshish. He went down to Joppa and found a ship bound for Tarshish; he paid his fare and went aboard, to go with them to Tarshish, to get away from Yahweh.

Jonah 1.1–3

A Palestinian monastic writer of the fifth century points out the sense of loss, foresakenness and abandonment by God [that] comes particularly to those men who are acting *contrary to the truth of their condition*:

> God does not abandon the negligent man who is negligent, nor the presumptuous man when he is presumptuous, but he abandons the devout man who becomes indifferent and the humble man when he is presumptuous. This is what is meant by sinning against one's condition. From this comes dereliction. (St Dorotheus of Gaza)

The price of this failure to measure up to an existential demand of one's own life is a general sense of failure, of guilt. And it is important to remark that *this guilt is real*, it is not necessarily a mere neurotic anxiety. *It is the sense of defection and defeat that afflicts those who are are not facing their own inner truth and are not giving back to life, to God and to their fellow human beings, a fair return for all that has been given them.*

Thomas Merton, *Contemplative Prayer* (DLT 1973), adapted

God may reduce you
on Judgement Day
to tears of shame
reciting by heart
the poems you would
have written, had
your life been good.

W. H. Auden

At times I think that I will be able to write one day, to describe things, but then I suddenly grow tired and say to myself, 'Why all these words?' I want every word I write to be born, truly born, none to be artificial, every one to be essential. For otherwise there is no point to it at all. And that is why I shall never be able to make a living by writing, why I must always have a job to earn my keep. Every word born of an inner necessity – writing must never be anything else.

Etty: A Diary 1941–43

The angel said to her, 'Mary, do not be afraid; you have won God's favour. Listen! You are to conceive and bear a son . . .'

Mary said to the angel, 'But how can this come about, since I am a virgin?' 'The Holy Spirit will come upon you', the angel answered, 'and the power of the Most High will cover you with its shadow. And so the child will be holy and will be called Son of God. Know this too: your kinswoman Elizabeth has, in her old age, herself conceived a son, and she whom people called barren is now in her sixth month, *for nothing is impossible to God.*' 'I am the handmaid of the Lord,' said Mary, 'let what you have said be done to me.' And the angel left her.

Luke 1.30–1, 34–8

A book stirs in me.

Elizabeth O'Connor, *Cry Pain, Cry Hope*

Even in the man there is motherhood, it seems to me, physical and spiritual; his procreating is also a kind of giving birth, and giving birth it is when he creates out of inmost fullness.

Rainer Maria Rilke, *Letters to a Young Poet*

I still have the particular vocation I had before – to be a 'people person', there for others, accessible and supportive when invited to be so. I do wonder whether in a curious way the being there for others (which I love) also means that God wants me to live alone (which I don't love).

So, I travel hopefully, not struggling any more against the solitude I so dreaded. I think I may at last have come to a sort of acceptance, provided I don't examine it too closely, that at least for the time being I am alone and that it is in many ways, like everything God has made, very good. It has at the very least made me more sensitive to the pain of loss and confusion felt by so many people, and has forced me to be more and more aware of my inner being. Silence in this part of Suffolk is silence indeed, especially at night, but it is no longer an empty silence. Sometimes it feels like a supreme gift I could no longer do without. So often when friends come into the cottage their first exclamation is 'Oh, how peaceful and welcoming!' If that peacefulness is really within my deepest self, and the ability to make others welcome continues to be one of the chief joys of my life, then perhaps I don't have to look further for a vocation to make itself clear.

Anthony Faulkner, *To Travel Hopefully* (DLT 1994)

God, take me by Your hand, I shall follow You dutifully, and not resist too much. I shall evade none of the tempests life has in store for me, I shall try to face it all as best I can. But now and then grant me a short respite. I shall never again assume, in my innocence, that any peace that comes my way will be eternal. I shall accept all the inevitable tumult and struggle. I delight in warmth and security, but I shall not rebel if I have to suffer cold, should You so decree. I shall follow wherever Your hand leads me and shall try not to be afraid.

I don't want to be anything special, I only want to try to be true to that in me which seeks to fulfil its promise.

Etty: A Diary 1941–43

The transition stage – the time between works – is often signaled by growing feelings of discontent. The work we have been doing ceases to absorb us in the same way. Finally it seems impossible to endure until the weekend, or vacation, or retirement. The period is one of anxiety, sometimes experienced as boredom. One reaches toward the new without knowing what the new is. The transition stage is a difficult period because the old has lost its meaning, the new has not yet loomed into sight, and one has serious doubts that it will come at all. These thoughts cause varying degrees of unrest and, in the extreme, despair. There is nothing to do but wait, and waiting is something few of us do well. We find ourselves, as it were, in exile. Only when looking back do we see that the pain was part of the design, seeking to pull us into the new. Pain kept us open in our waiting – asking, listening, looking, willing to make that journey into self – a journey few of us undertake with any seriousness until compelled by our suffering.

Elizabeth O'Connor, Cry Pain, Cry Hope

There is here no measuring with time, no year matters, and ten years are nothing. Being an artist means, not reckoning and counting, but ripening like the tree which does not force its sap and stands confident in the storms of spring without the fear that after them may come no summer. It does come. But it comes only to the patient, who are there as though eternity lay before them, so unconcernedly still and wide. I learn it daily, learn it with pain to which I am grateful: *patience* is everything!

Rainer Maria Rilke, Letters to a Young Poet

I am full of unease, a strange, infernal agitation, which might be productive if only I knew what to do with it. A 'creative' unease. Not of the body – not even a dozen passionate nights of love could assuage it. It is almost a 'sacred' unease. 'Oh God, take me into Your great hands and turn me into Your instrument, let me write.'

Etty: A Diary 1941–43

Each person, no matter how old, has an important work to do ... This good work not only accomplishes something needed in the world, but completes something in us. When it is finished a new work emerges that will help us to make green a desert place, as well as to scale another mountain in ourselves. The work we do in the world, when it is true vocation, always corresponds in some mysterious way to the work that goes on within us.

Elizabeth O'Connor, *Cry Pain, Cry Hope*

When we honor call in our lives, we honor it in the lives of others and of our institutions, for institutions – like people – journey by stages. They, too, must die to the old in order to be born to the new. The failure of an institution to follow its commitment to creativity causes it to wither and die – to become full of dead men's bones. A structure intended for the healing of the common life changes into a vehicle of oppression. Perhaps, when vocation becomes a more conscious consideration in our individual lives, it will become a more conscious consideration in our corporate life as the people of God called to freedom and creativity.

Elizabeth O'Connor, *Cry Pain, Cry Hope*

> O God for whom we long
> as a woman in labour
> longs for her delivery;
> give us courage to wait,
> strength to push,
> and discernment to know the right time;
> that we may each bring into the world
> the child you have given us to bear,
> through Jesus Christ.   Amen.

Janet Morley, *All Desires Known**

*Adapted by FD with permission. Original lines 7 and 8: 'that we may bring into the world/your joyful peace'. The reason for the change may be more fully understood by reading pages 127–9 of Francis Dewar, *Live for a Change*.

15

Fear and faintheartedness

There is no need to be afraid, little flock, for it has pleased your
Father to *give* you the Kingdom.
The Gospel of Luke

Of this process that I am offering you I have, of course, experienced
each facet myself – this one perhaps as much as any; for I am by
nature quite a timid person inside. My work involves, amongst
other things, running workshops of one kind or another on vocation and the calling of God. At the beginning of such an event with
a group or a crowd of people I have never met before, I can at times
be almost sick with nervousness and wonder why an earth I put
myself through this again and again; because it does not seem to get
any easier as I grow older. But once I have got started and begin to
make contact with the people and they with one another, I know
why. I absolutely love this work. It is such a privilege to see light
dawning and people beginning to discover what they are about.

Something to do

- Read the following verses from Isaiah and in place of the
  words Israel and Jacob insert your own name. Read it over
  slowly a few times. Hear God saying these words to you
  personally.

> You, [Israel,] my servant,
> [Jacob] whom I have chosen . . .
>
> You whom I brought from the confines of the earth
> and called from the ends of the world;
> you to whom I said, 'You are my servant,
> I have chosen you, not rejected you',
>
> do not be afraid, for I am with you;

stop being anxious and watchful, for I am your God.
I give you strength, I bring you help,
I uphold you with my victorious right hand . . .

For I, Yahweh, your God,
I am holding you by the right hand;
I tell you, 'Do not be afraid,
I will help you.'   Isaiah 41.8–10, 13

———— ◆ ————

[We realized] that doubt is a dimension that oftentimes is
there, and that there is a time to move on in spite of it. In fact,
we agreed that if anyone were too dogmatic about call, he
or she needed to question it because there is always the
possibility of acting out of some compulsive need rather than
genuine call. Frequently along with the call comes the feeling
that one is not up to it. There is a sense of unworthiness in
relationship to what one sees. 'Who am I to be called to bring
into existence anything so significant? Surely there are other
people more qualified to do it.' This is what Moses felt. He
was forever protesting that Yahweh could choose someone
better equipped for the job, someone who talked more con-
vincingly than he did. Jeremiah said flatly that he was too
young, even going to the extreme in that declaration, '"I am
only a child." But the Lord said, "Do not call yourself a
child; for you shall go to whatever people I send you and say
whatever I tell you to say."' (Exod. chs. 3 and 4; Jer. 1.6–7)

All of us resist in some way the new thing into which we
are drawn that demands a whole new dimension of creativity
on our part. We do not want to be responsible in this way.

Elizabeth O'Connor, Introduction to Gordon Cosby,
Handbook for Mission Groups

I don't know how to settle down to my writing. Everything is still much too chaotic and I lack self-confidence, or perhaps the urgent need to speak out. I am still waiting for things to come out and find a form of their own accord. But first I myself must find the right pattern, my own pattern.

Etty: A Diary 1941–43

O wait for the Lord, stand firm and he will strengthen your heart: and wait, I say, for the Lord.

Psalm 27.17 (ASB)

In the middle of November he moved in. But now he complained of prolonged rains, of inability to get to work, of waiting for the propitious hour, and how this waiting makes it always harder to begin, 'and the happiness of being a beginner, which I hold to be the greatest, is small beside the fear of beginning . . .'

M. D. Herder Norton, translator of Rilke's *Letters to a Young Poet*

Celebrate Christmas, dear Mr Kappus, in this devout feeling, that perhaps He needs this very fear of life from you in order to begin; these very days of your transition are perhaps the time when everything in you is working at him, as you have already once, in childhood, breathlessly worked at him. Be patient and without resentment and think that the least we can do is to make his becoming not more difficult for him than the earth makes it for the spring when it wants to come.

And be glad and confident.

Rainer Maria Rilke, *Letters to a Young Poet*

I acted the part all night, tormented by insomnia and the more I went through the lines the more I forgot them. During the day, in the street and in the carriage I wore myself out with the same relentless stupid repetition of the lines. During the day I was worn out, I lay down but could not sleep because I was still going through the lines. I arrived at the theatre completely exhausted. I made changes to the make-up in order to convince myself that I had discovered something and so give myself courage. I drank a double dose of drops and (horror of horrors) a secret glass of wine to cheer myself up . . .

My heart sank and I was in such total despair that I felt clumsy, superfluous, stupid, above all *ridicule*. God knows how I acted, I stumbled through the lines and almost came to a complete stop. The more I tried to overcome my apathy the more the audience coughed . . . With my inner plan in pieces I decided, in actors' jargon, to pull out all the stops, let fly physically and vocally. And did I not!! It was so easy but I knew that only sheer desperation could push me to such shameful lengths. The audience listened to me as never before. They even tried to applaud after the first scene. Moskvin rushed round during the interval and said that this was the only way to play it. I don't understand a thing.

Constantin Stanislavski quoted in Jean Benedetti, Stanislavski
(Methuen 1988)

One of the certain signs that we are at the periphery of our lives is our beginning to wonder whether or not what we are doing will be pleasing to others. Whenever we begin to act and produce with the approval of others in mind, there comes the haunting possibility that we will not live up to their actual or imagined expectations. To the degree that this feeling takes over we abandon ourselves, and spontaneity and creativity die in us.

Elizabeth O'Connor, Eighth Day of Creation

In the theatre, after desert-like wanderings and tortured exploration, plays are offered up in the hope that they create an experience of revelation. Terror grips the actors, directors, designers, as we offer each other the volatile conclusions of our work. Passions and tempers can run high. Vulnerabilities are released like flocks of crows. Sleep is lost. Aspiration and fear abound in equal measure. I myself often think of Gethsemane and wish the cup could pass from me as I stand ashen in the wings on the first night, where every step ahead seems like an abyss of hell.

Fiona Shaw, actress and broadcaster, in *Christian* (1994/3)

When I reflect deeply on my life and what I really want, it is not to be afraid. When I am afraid, I am miserable. I play it safe. I restrict myself. I hide the talent of me in the ground. I am not deeply alive – the depths of me are not being expressed. When I am afraid a tiny part of me holds captive most of me which rebels against the tyranny of the minority.

Gordon Cosby, in E. O'Connor, *Cry Pain, Cry Hope*

I was afraid, and I went off and hid your talent in the ground.

Matthew 25.25

As a writer . . . I have a vision of a work that might be healing, but I have no sense that I can bring it to completion. Also, somewhere along the way I begin to doubt the worth of what I want to say. After all, nothing is new under the sun. It has all been said before. And anyway, who am I to presume that others want me to share with them my heart and mind? Usually by sheer will power I overcome the enormous resistances in myself to begin a piece of writing. After that things fall into place. Thoughts are given, words flow and somewhere out of my sight a work of organization goes on. This does not mean that I do not still have an arduous piece of writing to do. Always I must keep throwing in my widow's mite.

This has to be true of the *new* that *anyone* is called to do. If the new work is not yet present, and therefore cannot be copied, or repeated, or reproduced, extraordinary effort is required.

Elizabeth O'Connor, Letters to Scattered Pilgrims

This word, 'You will not be overcome,' was said very distinctly and firmly to give us confidence and comfort for whatever troubles may come. He did not say, 'You will never have a rough passage, you will never be over-strained, you will never feel uncomfortable', but he *did* say, 'You will never be overcome.' God wants us to pay attention to these words, so as to trust him always with strong confidence, through thick and thin. For he loves us, and delights in us; so he wills that we should love and delight in him in return, and trust him with all our strength. So all will be well.

And then he vanished, and I saw no more.

Julian of Norwich, Revelations of Divine Love

There is no need to be afraid, little flock,
for it has pleased your Father to *give* you the Kingdom.

Luke 12.32

16

Get into action

However much you study, you cannot know without action.

Saadi of Shiraz

One of the ways I have found encouragement in my life is through what other people have written, or through stories that are our common human currency of communication. My main reason for attempting a book like this is the hope that you too will find a little help and guidance and encouragement from what others have written. This book was conceived as a companion volume to my *Live for a Change*. I had originally envisaged one quotation to a page throughout the whole book, even for the very short ones that are only a sentence or two. I felt each quotation needed to be uncluttered, to have lots of space round it, to encourage you to read it several times and turn it over in your mind, before going on to the next one. I felt that was particularly necessary in this chapter, where adjacent quotes, even on the same page (e.g. p. 158), are about completely different aspects of getting into action. Each quotation needs to be considered on its own for what it has to say; though there are instances where they are definitely intended to illuminate each other (e.g. on p. 152). However, to be publishable the whole book had to be drastically pruned and shortened, and the stories and quotations that remain have often had to be crowded together, not least in this chapter.

Nevertheless, even in its cut form, this section does give some idea of the variety of issues around getting into action; ranging from tentative exploratory steps, to what may be for you a great stride into a 'new land'. Getting into action may, for you, be a matter of trying some new things. After all, how can you know what you love to do without dipping a toe into a variety of pools? Or, at the other end of the scale, it could be for you a long way down the road, a deliberate and conscious response to a call from God and a willingness to live with the consequences.

So do not let your fears stop you. Try things. Be willing to make mistakes. Above all, do not try and trim the vision for fear of failure. It is sensible to weigh up the risks so that as far as possible you go into it with your eyes open; but it can be sinful to play safe. In my experience, if you are even vaguely along the lines God is beckoning you, his providence, his angels, his 'helpers' will mysteriously assist things to fall into place.

This does not mean you will not encounter problems: far from it. But it does mean that you will have a sense, at least some of the time, that the wind is behind you, however intractable the difficulties may seem. Whatever you do will not be without its flaws, just as no one of us is perfect. But for all its faults it will be a real gift to some.

Something to do

- If you have some idea of what God is calling you to, is there some step, however small, that you could take towards it? Usually only one step at a time is clear, and nothing will be clear beyond that step until you have taken it.
- If you do not have any awareness at all of God's calling to you, is there some task or activity that you would like to try, to see how you feel about it?

———◆———

After my husband died I felt lonely and useless. I just worked, got my money, and that was it. I felt like a zero.

So I thought: what can I give of myself? I called upon the Institute for the Blind, asking if my eyes could be of any use. Two days later they called me back, inviting me to dictate books to be written in Braille. They were schoolbooks. They wanted the blind kids to be included in the school programs with the other kids, so they needed somebody who could see to dictate.

The first impact was a shock. Two children came to get the papers. They were twins, and both were blind. They were not born blind; they became blind through being in an incubator with the wrong temperature after they were born, and this had burned their eyes. One boy was dark and the other fair. Very, very beautiful.

I hoped they wouldn't come anymore. It was too much. What struck me about these kids was their cheerfulness. All blind people there were cheerful.

I felt like a queen because I had eyes. I realized that I was lucky in spite of all that has happened to me. It was good for me to meet them. They even had a sculpture class working with clay. Once I saw them making vases with faces on them. The teacher would say, now touch your own chin, now touch your own nose. The next day I saw the most wonderful series of vases, one better than the other, each with a different face on it. I thought, what shouldn't we who have eyes accomplish if these people can do all this without eyes?

During the first days I remained shocked. I would close my eyes for a while and imagine what it is like to be blind. Then I began to feel rich. If you do something which you know from the start will not earn you anything, you feel extraordinarily rich. I don't think I do a great deal for them, and yet what I do feels good to me in my whole being.

Quoted in Piero Ferrucci, *What We May Be* (Turnstone 1982)

No one is able to judge her own work – to know its value or its lack of value. Michelangelo wrote in his journal, 'I am a poor man of little value, who keeps striving in that art which God has given me, to lengthen my life as much as I can.' After his years of exhausting work on the Sistine vault he commented simply in a letter to his father: 'I've finished that chapel I was painting. The Pope is quite satisfied.'

Elizabeth O'Connor, Cry Pain, Cry Hope

Some friends came by Flaubert's house on Friday to ask if he would join them on a weekend picnic. He said no, he was much too busy. They looked at his manuscript, made some small talk, and went on their way. On Sunday night they came back to say what a wonderful time they had had. They also asked Flaubert how his work had gone. He said that he had made enormous progress. So they looked at the manuscript again, and noticed that he was at exactly the same point as on Friday – in the middle of a sentence interrupted by a comma. They chided him for making no progress at all. He replied that they didn't understand – that he had, on Saturday changed the comma to a semicolon, and on Sunday changed it back to a comma; thus he had made wonderful progress.

Peter Stitt, The World's Hieroglyphic Beauty (Univ. of Georgia 1985)

In a recent essay in *The Christian Century*, Don Coville Skinner writes of Rosa Parks, who, thirty-two years ago, tired from a long day's work, tired of the tyranny that negated her humanity, refused to move to the back of a Montgomery, Alabama, bus. She was arrested, but by her simple act she ignited the civil rights movement. Recently she was given an award by Allegheny College.

The Allegheny College students' attitude appalled Skinner. They were unable to comprehend the significance of who she was or what she did. After an initially electric welcome, they became bored and wandered away because she failed to dazzle them.

> For those who remained in the chapel that evening, there was at least the possibility of seeing beyond hype and illusion to the redemptive potential of common things. Those who walked out may never understand. Awash in a sea of images at once artificial but marvelously entertaining, they have no tolerance for that which does not shock or distract or amuse.
>
> It is difficult to be hopeful about our future ... until we learn to appreciate a historical fact: the power of social change and the glue of social cohesion reside in the conviction of common people, not in the influence or rhetoric of charismatic leaders or cosmetic heroines. Leadership is vital, and I do not underrate it. As sunlight through a magnifying glass sets the grass ablaze, so leaders focus and direct the energies of a community. But the people are the sunlight, wherein resides the energy ...
>
> History knows no more awesome power, nor tyranny a more fearsome opponent, than ordinary acts of courage. In her stubborn refusal to be the victim of a degraded and degrading system, she provided an example for others, and the combination of these people's energies ignited the conscience of the nation, engulfing the institution of segregation.

Maggie Ross, *Pillars of Flame* (SCM, no date)

One of the commonest features of contemporary society is the feeling so many people have of being trapped by circumstances beyond their control. The universe is so vast. Human life is held by such a tenuous thread. The future is uncertain. The prospect of personal calamity is an ever present possibility, and death is the inevitable end to the short span of life which is everyone's lot . . .

The reaction of many people is to shrug their shoulders, turn their backs on what look like insoluble problems, and get on with their own domestic affairs, living for the present and hoping for the best . . . Those engaged in politics or social affairs in general talk of this attitude as apathy. But it is not caring about nothing. It is the attempt to escape from a public into a private world, which in the end proves self-defeating because no man can live to himself alone. However narrow the circle, society at large impinges upon it at every point. Escapism is a fool's paradise.

Paul Rowntree Clifford, Government by the People?

Personal holiness is not pursued in isolation from institutional struggle nor is institutional struggle allowed to become a kind of optional extra that those so minded can engage in as a spare time occupation, so long as it does not conflict with their real vocation, the pursuit of personal sanctification. Rather the one feeds on the other and both feed on the utter openness to the Spirit which I have called radical contemplation.

Charles Elliott, 'Structures, Sin and Personal Holiness',
Christian Faith and Political Hopes (Epworth 1979)

This is not the letter of confirmation that I promised you, and I do hope and pray that you will understand why.

When Andy and I came on the 'Live for a Change' course ... at the beginning of October, I was very much wrestling with God about the 1994 programme for the Vine. Part of me very much wanted to 'play safe' by asking people with a proven track record to come and lead days here; people who would be certain to draw in others by their name and reputation. At the same time I felt God was saying that was not the purpose for which he had called the Vine into being. There are other places ... which offer that, and there is very much a need for it. The Vine, however, is to be a far more low key operation, where very ordinary lay people 'minister' in a way to one another.

I was shown this very clearly last summer when a speaker let me down at the last minute, and we were thrown back upon the Holy Spirit, or our own resources, however one likes to put it. It was one of our most successful days, which people are still talking about. But it is fairly high risk, and I chickened out, and asked you to do a day next November. I knew at the time I was being disobedient, and I have felt uneasy ever since ... So please would you forgive me for messing you about in this way ... I enclose our 1994 Programme, from which you will see that I eventually managed, by the grace of God, to follow instructions! ...

Fi Radford, in a personal letter

You have to realize the appalling, frightening fact that you, as a human being, have to stand completely on your own feet; there are no scriptures, no leaders, nothing that can save you.

When you actually realize that fact, either you sink further in your corruption, or that very fact gives you tremendous energy to break through the network of the psychological structure of society – break through, shattering everything. And then you will never seek help, because you are free . . .

You have sought help politically, religiously from the gurus, socially in every way; they have all betrayed you. There have been revolutions – political and economic revolutions, communism, social revolutions. They are not the answers; they cannot help you, because they will bring more tyranny, more slavery.

It is only when you demand complete freedom and sustain that freedom that you will find, through an operational approach, reality, and it is that reality that will set [us] free – nothing else. And it is one of the most difficult things to realize that you have to stand completely alone, entirely by yourself.

It is only the [one] who is free who can co-operate. And it is the [one] who is free, who says: I will not co-operate.

Krishnamurti, *On Freedom*

Moses my servant is dead; rise – it is time – and cross the Jordan here, you and all this people with you, into the land which I am giving the people of Israel.

Joshua 1.2

Now having met together, they asked him, 'Lord, has the time come? Are you going to restore the kingdom to Israel?' He replied, 'It is not for you to know times or dates that the Father has decided by his own authority, but you will receive power when the Holy Spirit comes on you . . .'

As he said this he was lifted up while they looked on, and a cloud took him from their sight. They were still staring into the sky when suddenly two men in white were standing near them and they said, 'Why are you men from Galilee standing here looking into the sky?'

Acts 1.6–11a

From past experience I know that when I begin investing myself in a dream or in a life, the commitment grows. Where I put my energies and my treasure, my reluctant heart sometimes follows. If any of us had to be fully committed when starting out, very little would ever be begun. It would be like having to decide to marry on the first meeting. What we have to do is to take one step and, if it seems good, take another.

Elizabeth O'Connor, *Cry Pain, Cry Hope*

I am being driven forward
Into an unknown land.
The pass grows steeper,
The air colder and sharper.
A wind from my unknown goal
Stirs the strings
Of expectation.

Still the question:
Shall I ever get there?
There where life resounds,
A clear pure note
In the silence.

Dag Hammarskjöld, *Markings* (Faber & Faber 1966)

Moses sent them to reconnoitre the land of Canaan, 'Go up into the Negeb; then go up into the highlands. See what sort of country it is, and what sort of people the inhabitants are, whether they are strong or weak, few or many, what sort of country they live in, whether it is good or poor; what sort of towns they have, whether they are open or fortified; what sort of land it is, fertile or barren, wooded or open. Be bold, and bring back some of the produce of the country.'

At the end of forty days, they came back from their reconnaissance of the land. They sought out Moses, Aaron and the whole community of Israel, in the wilderness of Paran, at Kadesh. They made their report to them, and to the whole community, and showed them the produce of the country.

They told them this story, 'We went into the land to which you sent us. It does indeed flow with milk and honey; this is its produce. At the same time, its inhabitants are a powerful people; the towns are fortified and very big; yes, and we saw the descendants of Anak there. The Amalekite holds the Negeb area, the Hittite, Amorite and Jebusite the highlands, and the Canaanite the sea coast and the banks of the Jordan.'

Caleb harangued the people gathered about Moses: 'We must march in,' he said 'and conquer this land: we are well able to do it.' But the men who had gone up with him answered, 'We are not able to march against this people; they are stronger than we are.' And they began to disparage the country they had reconnoitred to the sons of Israel, 'The country we went to reconnoitre is a country that devours its inhabitants. Every man we saw there was of enormous size. Yes, and we saw giants there. We felt like grasshoppers, and so we seemed to them.'

At this, the whole community raised their voices and cried aloud, and the people wailed all that night. Then all the sons of Israel grumbled against Moses and Aaron, and the whole community said, 'Would that we had died in the land of Egypt, or at least that we had died in this wilderness! Why does Yahweh bring us to this land, only to have us fall by the sword, and our wives and young children seized as booty? Should we not do better to go back to Egypt?' And they said to one another, 'Let us appoint a leader and go back to Egypt.'

Numbers 13.17–20, 25–33; 14.1–4

Why am I so resistant to starting? Is it because I'm afraid of failing, of it not being what I want it to be? Perhaps so: because I have a deep longing in me to commit to paper a compilation which will encourage, enthuse and enliven people into discovering what they're for and offering it generously; but it's very unclear what form it will take, what shape it should have. I'm afraid to start, perhaps, because I fear it may be premature, a false start; it may begin to set the form too soon, to commit to paper a shape which is untrue, that will not contain and express the message. Once I start to do it *this* way, I feel I'm ruling out other ways which might have turned out to be better.

When I put these hesitations down in black and white my mind tells me that my worries are an illusion; 'why not try this way, and if it doesn't feel right, scrap it and try another?' That *sounds* sensible, but my heart whispers that it's not as easy as that. When with a marking knife you cut a straight line along the grain in a piece of pinewood and the knife strays off the line, it's quite difficult, with the errant groove in place, to cut a true line again.

Francis Dewar

The greatest deterrents to the potential of creativity in this world are the standards we impose on ourselves and on others, coupled with the failure to believe in our own uniqueness and our own powers.

Elizabeth O'Connor, *Cry Pain, Cry Hope*

Until one is committed, there is hesitancy; the chance to draw back: always ineffectiveness, concerning all acts of initiative and creation.

There is one elementary truth, the ignorance of which kills countless ideas and splendid plans: that the moment one definitely commits oneself, then providence moves too. All sorts of things occur to help one that would never otherwise have occurred. A whole stream of events issues from the decision, raising in one's favour all manner of unforeseen incidents and meetings and material assistance which no man could have dreamed would have come his way.

Whatever you can do, or dream you can, begin it: boldness has genius, power and magic in it.

Begin it now.

Goethe

If anyone asked me to define an artist or a prophet, I think that I would say that he is the one who dares to act on the bold belief that he has a word to speak that would be healing if it could be heard. Actually, all human beings way down deep hold this belief about themselves. The sorrow is that except for rare moments most of us are overcome by forces of disbelief. In time we cease to remember that our lives are for the greening of the earth and the greening of one another. We lose sight of the work we are to do, but the truth of it is hidden away in us, and makes call supremely important, lifting up as it does the healing dimension of true vocation.

Elizabeth O'Connor, *Cry Pain, Cry Hope*

My works are a celebration and a communion; I hope
something will happen between me and the audience, a transformation enabling people to understand something deep in
their guts, not just their minds.

If I am thinking of the wrong things, worrying about
technical problems, what the audience is thinking, trying to
'put it over', then it feels as though I am pushing against
something hard and inflexible, and *things fall apart*. But if I
stop trying, pay attention to what is happening in each
moment and allow the truth and meaning to flow through
me, there is time and space and *things fall together* without
effort.

As Joyce Grenfell said, 'If you can only get it quite clear
about being an instrument for joy to play through, then all is
taken care of.'

Peri Aston, solo theatre artist, in Christian (1994/3)

I used to grieve because I could not make reliably a close-
fitting lid for a canister, a teapot, a casserole. Sometimes the
lid fitted, sometimes it didn't. But I wanted it to fit. And I
was full of aggravation. Then a GI friend of mine who was
stationed in Korea sent me an ancient Korean pot, about a
thousand years old. I loved it at once, and then he wrote that
he thought I might like it because it looked like something I
might have made. Its lid didn't fit at all! Yet it was a museum
piece, so to speak. Why, I mused, do I require of myself what
I do not require of this pot? Its lid does not fit, but it inspires
my spirit when I look at it and handle it. So I stopped
worrying. Now I have very little trouble making lids that fit.

M. C. Richards, Centering in Pottery, Poetry, and the Person
(Wesleyan 1989)

There's a very strange phenomenon with which I have to live: the moment any performance is complete it is already of the past. I know that whatever preparation I've made for this 'Winter Journey' and its twenty-four songs is valid only until the evening of 15 November. After that, the journey goes on. The next interpretation will be different for a variety of small reasons of which I know nothing at present. Then that one will be gone, and so on, until I stop singing, I suppose.

Winterreise is harrowing, enlightening, perceptive. It's a work of such greatness that, like a Mozart opera, it can never pall. It's there in my being, now, and everything that happens to me will have a bearing on how I perform it next time.

Thomas Allen, *Foreign Parts: A Singer's Journal*
(Sinclair-Stevenson 1993)

When Ahab told Jezebel all that Elijah had done, and how he had put all the prophets to the sword, Jezebel sent a messenger to Elijah to say, 'May the gods do this to me and more, if by this time tomorrow I have not made your life like the life of one of them!' He was afraid and fled for his life. He came to Beersheba, a town of Judah, where he left his servant. He himself went on into the wilderness, a day's journey, and sitting under a furze bush wished he were dead. 'Yahweh,' he said 'I have had enough. Take my life; I am no better than my ancestors.' Then he lay down and went to sleep. But an angel touched him and said, 'Get up and eat.' He looked round, and there at his head was a scone baked on hot stones, and a jar of water. He ate and drank and then lay down again. But the angel of Yahweh came back a second time and touched him and said, 'Get up and eat, or the journey will be too long for you.' So he got up and ate and drank, and strengthened by that food he walked for forty days and forty nights until he reached Horeb, the mountain of God.

1 Kings 19.1–8

Last night Gordon Cosby talked to Sarah's Circle about fund-raising. He began by saying that he had met with a lot of groups discussing fund-raising, and that he finds without exception that their own attitude towards money is their greatest obstacle to raising it. He said, 'People working for the poor tend to treat money as the enemy. They resent having to raise it. The implication often is "We are laying down our lives for the poor – others ought to provide the money." We are all stuck in the materialism of our age. Very few people are free about money. Deal with your own ambivalence concerning it. Let your response to mission be wholistic – include your money as well as your time ... Be glad you are not starting out with money. When you have it you attract people who are looking for work and who want to make a career out of serving the poor. They see the project as a way of breaking into the political arena. When you have money people want jobs with you for the salaries they will receive and the careers they will further. When you have no money there is no mistaking who is called.'

Elizabeth O'Connor, Cry Pain, Cry Hope

What stirs in our hearts will never correspond with what we are able to transpose onto paper or canvas or to shape into bridges and buildings and highways and institutions. Trying is all that matters. Our yes to call is saying that we will try. The guide, helper, angel, mentor, or, if you prefer, 'the little fellow of the wood – some wizard, hermit, shepherd, or smith' – will appear, to supply the amulets and advice.

When the book is written, or the institution built, it will fall short, no matter how much blood it costs. Then there is nothing to do but write another book, paint another picture, start another project, dream another dream, see another vision. If it has to do with the lifting up of valleys and the leveling of mountains, the supernatural aid will be given again.

Elizabeth O'Connor, *Cry Pain, Cry Hope*

O God our dance,
in whom we live and move and have our being;
so direct our strength
and inspire our weakness
that we may enter with power
into the movement of your whole creation,
through our partner Jesus Christ, Amen.

Janet Morley, *All Desires Known*

Something further to do

• At this point you could look back over all the stories and quotations in this book and from each chapter choose just one story or one quote that particularly registers with you or that somehow stands out for you. You don't have to explain to yourself *why* a particular piece strikes you, just notice that it does. When you have chosen your sixteen pieces, keep them by you for a time and turn them over in your mind. In the case of a story, ask yourself where you are in it. For example, for the last few years a favourite of mine has been the Iranian fairy-tale on page 32. At the present time I feel like the prince wandering in the desert. It's not a surface feeling; I'm very happy and contented and fulfilled at one level. It's more an underlying feeling, which I could easily ignore in the busyness of daily life. At other times I have experienced other facets of that story. It is a very fruitful one for me just now.

  In a similar way the stories and quotes *you* choose have something to convey to you about where you are. They do not necessarily say anything about where you *will* be, but they do have something to say about your feelings at present, if you will take the time to listen. And where you are now is the only starting point for the next stage of your journey. Strangely, it can be quite difficult to start from where you are. How easy it is to want to start from somewhere else; or to kid yourself that you are other than you are; or to think that you are *supposed* to be other than you are and that the 'true' starting place is somewhere else!

  So, for now, occupy the 'place' where you are and savour it. Even if it is not to your liking, it is the base camp from which you must set out.

17

Helpers and guides

A patron is much more fundamental than we thought...patron being defined as 'one chosen, named, or honoured as a special guardian, protector, supporter, or the like'.   Elizabeth O'Connor

Do not be misled by the fact that, like Gideon in Judges, chapter 6, this section is one of the smallest in this little family of seventeen. In the matter of the discernment of God's calling to you the guidance and feedback of others is not an option; it is *essential*. Otherwise, one or other of the twin ogres of low self-esteem or invincible arrogance are liable to take possession of you, or just plain deluded nuttiness. It is mainly the first two which lie in wait for those of us who seek to discover what God wants us to do. Their disguises, as 'humility' or 'confidence in God', are not possible to penetrate without the help of a wise, perceptive and godly friend. That is the function of what in traditional language is called spiritual direction, which is outlined in the first three quotations. But also needed, at a lower, preliminary level, as it were, is a wider form of what Elizabeth O'Connor calls patroning. We all, however able we may appear to others, need someone to affirm what we are, to identify, draw out and encourage our gifts and capabilities. We can do this for each other in all kinds of ordinary, daily ways, for example by letting someone know that they have done something well.

I leave out of account here the need most of us have at some time or another for counselling or for coming to terms with what we see as problems or disabilities. We took some note of that in chapter 7.

Something to do

- Do you have a spiritual director or godfriend, such as Jim Cotter (p. 163) describes? How about taking steps to find one?

- Look back over the past month. Have there been instances when you have felt affirmed by someone for something you have done? Have you affirmed another person's capability? What did you say or do? How was it received?

———— ✦ ————

We are so clumsy, so deaf, so blind because of our passions and egotism that we easily deceive ourselves in regard to what the Spirit wishes to say to us. We need to have it confirmed by a voice other than our own.

A Carthusian, *The Way of Silent Love* (DLT 1993)

We need companions on the journey, those who may be *god-friends* to us (on the analogy of godmothers and godfathers), friends who help to keep us to a chosen narrow way of pilgrimage, who themselves are becoming *friends of God*. This is not easy, and we need the warning of Gregory of Nazianzen that we should 'be, rather than seem to be, the friends of God'.

Such friendship is usually askew, in the sense that the one is there for the other, but not the other way round. This can allow the process of review to be clear and uncluttered. If some find that they can change roles in a mutual giving and receiving, they need a third person from time to time to make sure that the blind are not leading the blind in mutual cosiness – there is a tough streak to discernment.

It also needs to be said that this process is not the same as therapy or counselling – though sensitivities learned in those activities can be helpful. The occasion of review may however reveal a need for such counselling. 'Noise' from the emotional past can interfere with the deeper tuning on the longer wavelengths that characterizes spiritual discernment.

Jim Cotter, circular letter

Crises occur at those points where we see how unreality, our selfish, self-protecting illusions, our struggles for cheap security, block the way to our answering the call to be. To live like this, to nurture and develop this image of myself, may be safe, but it isn't true: insofar as it's unreal it's un-Godly. God cannot reach me if I'm not there.

And so the crisis comes when we put the question, 'What am I denying, what am I refusing to see in myself? What am I trying to avoid?' This is where we have to begin really to attend, to ourselves and to the world around, to find out what is true and what is false in us. Not just introspection, because we don't just live in private selves . . .

[We need to be asked] 'Have you reckoned with *that* aspect of yourself, with *that* feature of your relationships? Is this actually *you* we've got here? Or is it another defence, another game?' . . .

Our hearts are infinitely cunning in self-deceit; we need others to let the cold light of accuracy shine on our evasions and posturing. All of us have to ask one another at times; 'Tell me who you think I am' and all of us are obliged to answer that with as much candour – and as much charity – as we can. Someone's life depends on it.

Rowan Williams, *Open to Judgement*

Very few of us have had a listening, seeing person in our lives. We do not hear what others – not even our children – are saying because we, ourselves, have had no one to hear us. We do not have the feeling that what we think and what we say is important.

Many of us make this confession to one another in the small groups of The Church of The Saviour when we struggle to identify and exercise our gifts. Such confession helps to dispel one's illusion that he is the only one who lacks confidence and needs confirmation. We begin to see that our need is everyman's need and that the person who looks so assured and confident and collected is hardly ever what he appears to be. He wears for us the same mask that we wear for him. If we think about it, we know that the reason that he did not give us the confirmation we were seeking is because he was too busy trying to find confirmation for himself. As for us, we could not answer his plea, so concerned were we with our own place in the scheme of things.

When this happens in a group, we do not have Christian community or any other kind of community. We may be sitting in a circle in the same room, but each of us is living in a separate world revolving around himself. And what we hear and see is in terms of ourselves, which is to see or hear hardly at all. To be a person in community one must both give and receive, confirm and be confirmed. The Christian Church comes into being as we come to know our own gifts and help others to know theirs.

Elizabeth O'Connor, Eighth Day of Creation

My light is burning bright;
My stride is long, my head is high.
Don't go; I need the humility of your low light.
Stay near and, if by chance you see more clearly to
    take your next few steps,
We shall have served each other well.

But now my light is glimmering low.
I stumble and barely see the way.
I need your light which now is burning strong.
Dare I believe you still need mine?

And now my light is out, I think;
I cannot find the way at all
But stand in darkness, lost, afraid . . .
Until I see your light, and trust your reassuring hand,
And strength returns, and fear has gone.

And now again, somehow, my light is burning bright.
Yet I did not *see* your light touch mine.
We are a gift and a miracle, you and I . . .

Derek Corlett

A religious order founded in the seventeenth century, which
at one time flourished, with many houses all over the country, had shrunk to five elderly monks occupying a cavernous
house in acres of grounds. For many years they had had no
enquiries from people wanting to join the order. They were
downhearted and turned in on themselves.

One day they had a request from a local rabbi. Could he
be allowed the occasional use of an empty cottage situated in
their woodland grounds for periods of quiet and retreat?
They gladly agreed, pleased to be asked.

Some weeks later, when the rabbi was using the cottage,
the abbot made a courtesy call to see that everything was all
right for him. They got talking, and found they had quite a
lot in common in bemoaning the lack of religious commitment
these days. The abbot asked the rabbi if he had any advice to
offer about how to rekindle the life of his community. The
rabbi said he wished he knew: all he could say was, 'One of

your community members is the Messiah.' The abbot thought to himself, 'Well I never! Rabbis are renowned for their pithy sayings, but this one is surely a little over the top.'

Back at the monastery in the recreation time that evening the other monks wanted to know how the conversation had gone. The abbot told them what the rabbi had said. They looked at one another in astonishment for a second or two before bursting out laughing, 'What a stupid idea! He must be off his trolley.'

But, ridiculous though it sounded, the thought somehow kept coming back to each of them as they went about their activities in the days that followed. Could he mean the abbot? He's certainly been abbot for a long time and he is a fair-minded man; but he isn't exactly one to set the world on fire. Perhaps he'd meant Brother Henry. Henry is quite a holy man: everyone knows that, though he is a bit dull. Could he be the one? It couldn't be Brother William. He's the awkward Yorkshireman who always stirs up trouble by speaking his mind. But you have to admit he often says things that need saying. He certainly couldn't have meant Brother Aidan. He is a real doormat, a non-entity if ever there was one. Though he does seem to have a knack of being there when you need him. He just seems to appear at the right moment. Of course the rabbi couldn't have meant me. I'm nothing special; really, I'm just an ordinary person. Oh God, not me! You couldn't ask that of me. Could you?

As each of them turned these thoughts over in their minds, they began to treat each other with a great deal more respect, on the off-chance that one of them might be the Messiah. Their appreciation and expectations of each other began to grow.

The beautiful grounds in which the monastery was set had always been used occasionally by picnickers and walkers but these casual visitors began to be aware of a different feel about the place. They began to visit the house itself and the chapel, curious to know more. After a time, there came the occasional enquiry about the order itself and how one might join. Within a year two postulants had joined the order. In the years that followed, the community began to thrive, and once again became a centre of light and spiritual power.

Acknowledgements

In a compilation like this thanks are due to a great many people, not least the authors whose words I have quoted, variously for their wisdom, their spiritual perceptiveness, their clarity, their humanity, and for their way with words.

I am grateful also

to David Wood, Penny Wright, Terry Nottage, Mary Wilson, Carol Simmons, Gwen Cashmore and Joan Puls, Graham Pigott, and Fi Radford who drew my attention to pieces I have quoted.

to Simon Baynes, Ann Lewin, Janet Morley, Jim Cotter, Charles Handy, Derek Corlett, and above all Elizabeth O'Connor, who gave me their personal permission to quote copyright material.

for permission to quote:– *The Jerusalem Bible* © 1966 by Darton Longman & Todd and Doubleday & Co. Inc. (all translations of biblical material are from the JB unless otherwise indicated); *Open to Judgement* by Rowan Williams (DLT 1994); *Etty: A Diary 1941–43* (Jonathan Cape 1983); the poem 'God ran away' from *I hear a seed growing* by Edwina Gateley (Anthony Clarke Publishers, UK, and Source Books Ca., USA, 1990); 'Murder in the Cathedral' by T. S. Eliot (*The Complete Poems and Plays of T. S. Eliot*, Faber & Faber 1969); the lines 'God may reduce you on judgement day' by W. H. Auden (Faber & Faber); *Doorways to Christian Growth* by Jacqueline McMakin with Rhoda Nary (Winston Press 1984); the poem 'The Musician' by R. S. Thomas (*Collected Poems of R. S. Thomas*, J. M. Dent 1993) used by permission of Gwydion Thomas; *Journey Inward, Journey Outward* by Elizabeth O'Connor (Harper & Row 1968) used by permission of Harper Collins Publishers Inc..

to Diana Gordon Clark, Fi and Andy Radford, Elizabeth Dewar, Charles Foister, Mary Lewis, Mary Wilson and David Wood who read all or part of this book in draft and made critical and helpful suggestions.

to Rachel Boulding, my editor at SPCK, who did the midwifery, and Lizzi Gill who did much of the typing.

Every effort has been made to trace sources and obtain permission from copyright holders of material quoted here. Information on any omissions should be sent to the publishers, who will make full acknowledgement in any future edition.

Please note that *Cry Pain, Cry Hope* by Elizabeth O'Connor is now published by The Servant Leadership School, 1640 Columbia Road NW, Washington DC 20009, USA, and is obtainable from there.

Notes on authors quoted more than once

Anthony Bloom, 1914–2003. Archbishop of the Orthodox Church in Britain, and writer on prayer.

Paul Rowntree Clifford, 1913–2003. President of Selly Oak Colleges, and writer on Christianity and society.

Gordon Cosby. As a North American Baptist minister he was a chaplain in the 101st Airborne Division in France in the Second World War. That experience changed his life, and he founded The Church of the Saviour in Washington DC in 1946, which is a kind of lay, dispersed, religious order, whose whole rationale is the living of personal calling.

Jim Cotter. Anglican priest, counsellor, writer of prayers and of books on sexuality, healing and Christian ministry.

Matthew Fox. North American former Dominican, now an Episcopalian, who has done much to interpret and popularize the teaching of Meister Eckhart, a Dominican who lived in the fourteenth century.

Frederick Franck, 1909–2006. Artist and author of books on drawing and on religion. Worked with Albert Schweitzer for three years.

John Howard Griffin. Novelist, photographer and social activist. His best known book is *Black Like Me*. He was appointed Thomas Merton's official biographer, but died in 1980 before completing it.

Paul Harrison. Journalist and writer on poverty and deprivation.

Hermann Hesse, 1877–1963. German novelist and poet. Earned condemnation by the Nazis for his pacifism and opposition to German militarism. Awarded the Nobel Prize for Literature in 1946.

Etty Hillesum. She was a Dutch Jew who kept a wartime journal from 1941 to 1943, first in Holland and latterly in Westerbork Camp, to which she went voluntarily in 1943 to share in the fate of the Jewish people. She was incredibly honest and perceptive, and the book movingly describes her gradual discovery and living of her personal calling, in the end in the most appalling circumstances. It is a classic, one of the best articulations of the journey of personal calling that I know. She died in Auschwitz on 30 November 1943, aged 28.

Julian of Norwich, c.1342–c.1416. Anchoress and mystic.

Carl Gustav Jung, 1875–1961. Polymath, sage and intrepid explorer of the inner life of the human race. He was associated with Freud in his early working life, but broke away from him in 1914 to pursue his own researches. He developed a system of psychology broader and deeper than Freud's, which is at last becoming better known and understood.

Brian Keenan. Held hostage in Beirut for four-and-a-half years in the late 1980s. *An Evil Cradling* is an account of that experience.

Jiddhu Krishnamurti, 1896–1986. 'Discovered' as a boy of 15 in India in 1910 by the Theosophists, Krishnamurti was groomed by them as a sort of messiah, a role he eventually rejected. He became a spiritual teacher who refused to play the guru.

Thomas Merton, 1915–68. Became a Trappist monk in 1941 at the Abbey of Gethsemani in Kentucky. He lived the search for an authentic life as a monk, as a writer and as a Christian committed to peace and justice issues. His life was an example of the struggle towards personal vocation within a religious community, and of the problems of authority and integrity that that involved.

Arnold and Amy Mindell. The Mindells have developed a practical therapeutic method called process work which helps people to integrate the spiritual, emotional, psychological and physical aspects of their nature and personal history.

Janet Morley. Worked for more than a decade with the Churches' Team at Christian Aid. She is now Secretary for Adult Learning at the Methodist Church, and a writer of prayers and liturgies.

Nasrudin. Not an author so much as a character who appears in various guises in stories, e.g. as mullah, sage, villager, joker, idiot and drawer of attention to human foibles and follies. The Turks allege that he actually lived in the thirteenth century and make a tourist attraction of a festival in his honour.

Friedrich Nietzsche, 1844–1900. Philosopher and writer. *Thus Spoke Zarathustra* is a powerful and curious explosion of a book.

Henri Nouwen, 1932–96. Dutch Roman Catholic priest, university teacher and writer on the spiritual life, who lived and worked in the L'Arche community in Toronto.

Elizabeth O'Connon, died 1998. From 1953 she was a staff member of The Church of the Saviour in Washington DC (*see also* Gordon Cosby). She wrote many books, and through them has been a kind of mentor to me.

M. Scott Peck, 1936–2005. Psychotherapist and writer on community-building.

Mary Caroline Richards, 1916–99. 'When people asked me what I did, I was uncertain what to answer; I guessed I could say I taught English, wrote poetry, and made pottery. What was my occupation? I finally gave up and said "person".'

Rainer Maria Rilke, 1875–1926. German poet. He was sent by his parents to a military academy, where he was like a fish out of water. Through many struggles he discovered his vocation as a poet. The ten letters from which the quotations are taken were written when he was in his late twenties.

Jalaludin Rumi. Born in Afghanistan in 1207, died in Turkey in 1273. Sufi sage, 'teacher' and writer.

Saadi of Shiraz, 1184–1263. Classical Sufi author.

Stories. If you want to know the authorship of the stories in this collection I have to disappoint you. Stories have a way of being not 'by' any individual. They change in each retelling. They are, or at least the 'good' ones become, communal. In each case, I suppose, someone must have been the first to articulate the germ or basic idea of a story. But the clothing is furnished each time by the teller. To adapt slightly the title of one of Rumi's books 'You get out of it what is in it for you'. That goes for the hearer as well as the teller.

Simone Weil, 1909–43. Teacher of philosophy, manual worker, mystic. She was a kind of patron saint of integrity. She had always had delicate health and her death in England was a result of her refusal to allow herself more rations than her compatriots were having to live on in occupied France.

Rowan Williams. Archbishop of Canterbury. Theologian and preacher.